CONTENTS

INTRODUCTION

Growing plants has always been an abiding interest of the British people. Even when the provision of food and medicine has been the primary concern, a wide range of decorative plants has also been grown and enjoyed. When plants no longer had to be grown for food, they were grown for fun.

The Romans brought many plants from their homeland when they settled in Britain, and the remains of their villas show evidence of decoratively laid out, formal gardens. Medicinal plants and herbs for flavouring were common imports. Some of these native Mediterranean plants failed to thrive in the colder, sunless British Isles, but many did adapt, and persisted even after the Romans had left and the country fell into the Dark Ages.

By the Middle Ages, monasteries had extensive herb gardens which were important for their medicinal plants.

From that time on, we know quite a lot about the great gardens surrounding the castles and stately homes of the country but less about the common man's garden around his cottage. We do know that there were many fashions, including the famous 'Tulipmania' of the seventeenth century, when bulbs changed hands for unbelievable sums of money. Other 'show' plants such as auriculas and pinks also became much sought after and were very valuable for a short while. For the majority of the population, however, gardening was simply a matter of growing vegetables and fruit to feed the family and flowers to add a little pleasure and beauty to an otherwise fairly grim existence.

A wide range of gardening tools and implements, some very specialized, has been used throughout the history of gardening. The main aim of most tools, of course, was to save labour: to find easier ways of doing heavy or mundane jobs. Some have persisted until the present day in more or less the same form while others

GARDENING AS IT WAS

Jane Courtier

B T Batsford Ltd, London

First published 1995

Printed and bound in Great Britain by
Butler & Tanner Ltd, Frome and London

for the Publisher

B. T. Batsford Ltd
4 Fitzhardinge Street
London
W1H 0AH

A catalogue record for this book is available from
the British Library

ISBN 0 7134 7368 1

8/12

635.094

GARDENING AS IT WAS

have disappeared altogether, perhaps because they were too specialized, too complicated, ineffective or simply replaced by something better.

In 1884, the newspaper *Amateur Gardening* first appeared. It was different because it was written not for the Head Gardeners of the large country estates, but for the owners of smaller, suburban and city gardens who would actually carry out much of the work themselves. It was a down-to-earth, practical publication which soon built up a loyal readership of gardeners who were not only willing to learn but also to pass on the results of their experiences to other readers. From the first issues of the paper, it is possible to feel a real empathy with the gardeners of the day, with their troubles and their triumphs.

As soon as manufacturers realized the type of readership *Amateur Gardening* had, they were not slow to begin advertising their wares. Some products are easily identifiable as the forerunners of those that have proved useful over the years; others looked promising but for some reason never caught on; while some now seem wildly eccentric.

Amateur Gardening carried its readers through many world-shattering events, including two world wars. It is a fascinating exercise to look back through the years.to see how the great topics of the time were reflected in its pages and to see how many things have changed in the world of gardening — and how many have not.

It has been difficult to select only a few items from such a wealth of material, but I have tried to find those that give a real flavour of their time, and that are interesting and entertaining. I hope my selection will enable you, too, to share this fascinating world of gardeners over the last century.

1884–1918

Gardening in the Victorian age conjures up pictures of country estates with vast grounds looked after by a bevy of employees, headed by a fearsome and very knowledgeable Head Gardener. But of course this is not the complete story. As well as the country estates there were numerous small gardens attached to town houses and suburban villas, and while the owners may have employed a part-time gardener, they undertook most of the work in the garden themselves. In 1884 a new gardening paper appeared: it was called *Amateur Gardening*, and as the title implies, it was for 'a class of persons who prefer attending personally to the management of their own gardens'. A glance through some of the early editions shows that many of the problems and difficulties that faced the Victorian gardener are just the same as those we face today — but the army of remedies and tools we have to help overcome the problems are rather different.

For much of the period from the first edition of *Amateur Gardening* to the beginning of the Great War in 1914, a labourer's weekly wage was around £1, making some of the prices for garden equipment and sundries seem very high. Once the First World War was under way, the shortage of manpower pushed the labourer's weekly wage up to £4, where it stayed for some considerable time. The shortage of labour would have made it even more necessary for the garden owner to carry out the work in the garden himself.

Garden tools

One of the most significant inventions as far as gardeners are concerned must be that of the lawn mower in 1830. Before then, 'lawns' had been very different, being areas of grass kept short first by flocks of sheep, then by men with scythes. Scything was a skilful job, but even the most skilled of men could not hope to produce as velvet-smooth a sward as those that were to become popular following Budding's invention of the lawn mower.

The inspiration for the lawn mower is thought to have come from the equipment used in textile mills to shear the nap on cloth. It was an invention that was to become quickly successful and there were soon several makes of lawn mower available, all claiming superiority of design. Ease of use was a major selling point, some manufacturers pointing out their machine could be used not only by men but by ladies too 'who are able to enjoy the light exercise its use entails'.

As lawns grew in popularity, complex flower beds and borders were cut out of them, making many yards of lawn edges to cope with. The Front Runner mower (May 1915, page 55) incorporated a small wheel to support the machine when mowing right to the edge of a verge, while the Adies lawn edger (May 1891, page 30) consisted of automatic shears attached to a roller. This was claimed to be 'as great an advance on the old shears as the lawn mower was over the scythe'. Grass boxes to collect the clippings were generally an optional extra. For larger areas of grass, pony-drawn mowers were available.

Although mechanical cultivators were still a long way off, improved ways of tilling the soil were already in evidence. Gamages Cultivator Hoe (June 12 1912) is of a design that has stood the test of time right up to the present day, while the No.7 Hand Wheel Cultivator (1912, page xv) was advertised as a remedy for back-ache. It was claimed to hoe, cultivate, rake, earth up, open furrows etc. in a third of the time.

Standard garden tools such as spades and forks were not widely advertised, but 'Sheffield-made' was a mark of quality (July 13 1907, page 142). A keen gardener was expected to have a full set of cultivation tools, and was encouraged to make a 'novel and exceedingly useful' tool rack and compost bin (February 23 1897, page 399) as a 'pleasant occupation during the long winter evenings.'

The New Plant Barrow (February 14 1885, page 493) enabled one man to 'move from place to place large and heavy plants'. The wide wheels were to prevent damage to garden paths.

Boby's Handy Seed Drill (1912, page 17) speeded up the sowing of large quantities of seeds, and was available in varying sizes to suit different sized seeds. The problems of root disturbance when transplanting were overcome with Richards Transplanting Implements (November 7 1896, page 276).

Secateurs were a French invention that had largely replaced knives for many pruning jobs, but the best of both worlds was combined in a pocket tool from Hill & Son (July 13 1912, page iii).

THE "EASY" LAWN MOWER.

Has an
OPEN STEEL ROLLER.

A lady can work a
20 inch
and a man a
30 inch Machine,
cutting grass 5 inches
high clean to its roots.

Before ordering
elsewhere send for
List to your

There is
No Easier
Working,
No Better
Finished,
No Stronger,
No more
Durable Mower
in the Market.

Ironmonger or
Seedsman, or to the
Sole Licensees

TRADE
MARK

SELIG, SONNENTHAL & CO.,
85, Queen Victoria Street, London, E.C.

(MAY 14 1887)

"ADIES" LAWN EDGER
OR
AUTOMATIC SHEARS,
PATENTED.

Awarded (after trial) Banksian Medal and Certificate of
Merit of the Royal Horticultural Society.

THIS INVENTION consists of a pair of Shears,
attached to a small roller, which work automatically, and will cut the grass edges as fast as
it is possible to push the machine along.

"We know not which to admire most, its
simplicity or efficiency. It is as great an advance
on the old Shears as the Lawn Mower was over
the Scythe."—*The Journal of Horticulture.*

OF ALL IRONMONGERS, FLORISTS & SEEDSMEN.
Price, complete, **21/-,**
Or will be sent carefully packed on receipt of P.O.O. **22/-**
to 13, CHARTERHOUSE STREET, LONDON, E.C.

(MAY 1891)

RANSOMES'
Inventions Exhibition, 1885,
SILVER MEDAL.
For "NEW AUTOMATON" MOWER.

LAWN MOWERS.
IMPORTANT NOVELTIES FOR 1886.

"NEW AUTOMATON"... The best Gear Machine.
"CHAIN AUTOMATON" The best Chain Machine.
"NEW PARIS" ... ... The best Small Machine.

All Mowers sent on a Month's Trial, Carriage Paid.
Stock in London at Arch 92, Spitalfields Station,
Bethnal Green. Orders executed promptly by all
Ironmongers. Write for Price List of these and of
the New Patent LAWN EDGE CUTTER, to

RANSOMES, SIMS, & JEFFERIES, LTD., IPSWICH.

(JULY 1886)

GAMAGE'S
CULTIVATOR HOE.

THE
ESSENTIAL
TOOL
FOR THE
SMALLHOLDER

Head made entirely of steel.

Light, well-made,
serviceable.

With 4½ foot handle.

Two prongs changeable for rows of any width. Loosening nuts, releases the prong.
Works between rows of centre prong can be removed and rows straddled. A
perfect weeder and pulveriser, giving level cultivation. Removing centre prong and
reversing other four, makes Potato Digger.

Five Prongs	each	**2/11**
Three Prongs	„	**1/11½**
Three Fixed Steel Prongs	„	**1/7**

CARRIAGE EXTRA.

OUR LATEST AWARD.—Silver-Gilt Banksian Medal (highest award) for Garden Tents,
Chairs, Shelters and Lawn Mowers————————for third year in succession.

A. W. GAMAGE, Ltd., Holborn, London, E.C.

(JUNE 12 1912)

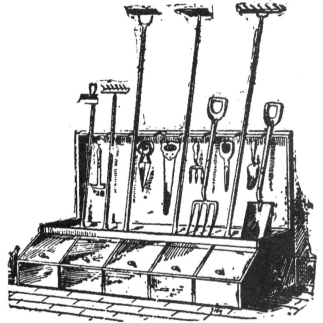

FIG. 1.—TOOL RACK AND COMPOST BIN.

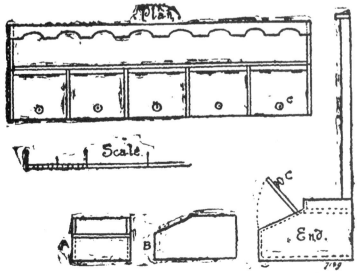

FIG. 2.—SECTION OF TOOL RACK AND COMPOST BIN.

(FEBRUARY 23 1897)

The New Plant Barrow here figured will enable one man to remove from place to place large and heavy plants. By slightly raising the handle, the back part of the board will come in contact with the ground, thus allowing a pot very easily to be placed on the centre. The wheels are made with wide tyres to prevent damage to garden paths. The manufacturers are Brangwin, Ridley and Co., Paragon Works, Hackney, E.

The late Mr. George Bentham, the celebrated botanist, has bequeathed the sum of £1,000 each to the Linnæan Society and the Royal Society Scientific Relief Fund, and the residue of his estate, after the payment of legacies to his relatives, executors, trustees, servants and others, is to be held upon trust to apply the same in preparing and publishing botanical works, or in the purchase of books or specimens for the botanical establishment at Kew.

(FEBRUARY 14 1885)

Greenhouses

The great plant hunters of the Victorian era sent vast numbers of previously unknown specimens to the British Isles from a wide range of countries — America, China, Japan, Australia and India — where growing conditions were very different from those at home. Glasshouses, where warmth and shelter could be provided, were necessary to keep the newcomers alive (though even in these many did not survive for long). For the keen gardener, a greenhouse became essential to grow some of the exciting new varieties that were becoming available to the general public. On the estates of wealthy landowners, greenhouses and conservatories were often vast, ornate structures, but many simpler, cheaper designs supplied ready to be erected by 'any gardener or handy-man' were also on the market.

The conservatory was, as it is today, an extension of the living rooms of the house and a place for social gatherings; but plants played a much more important part then they do in many modern conservatories. They were arranged for decorative effect on the staging and also in beds, with their pots sunk level with the soil.

The type of structure illustrated in the advertisement of Messenger & Co. (1889, page 59) was unlikely to be within reach of the majority of *Amateur Gardening* readers, but the manufacturers promise special attention given to amateurs' greenhouses, which can be 'readily put up, and removed without taking out any glass'. Richardson's horticultural buildings (August 7 1886, page iv) could be fixed 'in any part of the kingdom with Hot Water Apparatus complete'. Coopers Greenhouses (October 17 1896, page viii) are not modest about the virtues of their buildings: 'without doubt the cheapest, most complete, simplest to erect and best value for money in the trade.' A 7ft by 5ft span-roof greenhouse cost £2 16s in 1897. They could also supply you with an iron church, temporary hospital or bungalow, all despatched by rail (November 13 1897, page viii).

The majority of conservatories and greenhouses were still ornate: even the functional-sounding melon and cucumber frames of Geo. Dawson (1885, page 324) were highly decorative. Sendall's lean-to (June 1896, page viii), however, was of a much plainer style.

Those who hankered after a conservatory but did not have the necessary space or money could perhaps have made do with a cheaper option — a window conservatory (1885, page 547). Although suitable for an attractive display of a few plants, it was a poor substitute for the real thing.

Heaters

If a greenhouse was to be really useful for the growing of unusual tender plants it had to be heated during the winter. 'Heating the greenhouse appears to be an inexhaustable problem' *Amateur Gardening* complained in 1886, but there also appeared to be an inexhaustable supply of heaters suitable for every conceivable purpose.

The Loughborough Boiler (October 18 1884, page 289) did not require a separate boiler house but was fixed in the wall of the greenhouse so that it could be fuelled and attended to from outside, avoiding dust and a 'dry, killing atmosphere' among the plants. Ivanhoe boilers (December 20 1884, page 397) and Fawke's Slow-combustion heaters (January 16 1886, page 445) were designed on the same principle, and were said to be well adapted for small houses. Christy's Crescent heaters (November 1884, page 372) used just a paraffin lamp as a heat source: the crescent-shaped pipe provided heat very rapidly.

For small greenhouses, a portable heating system was far more appropriate than fixed boilers and pipes. Poore's Challenge Heating Apparatus (January 3 1885, page 433) used a portable oil, gas or coke heater instead of a boiler: the pipes could also be moved around the greenhouse as required. The warm air was said to be 'perfectly sweet and wholesome'.

In 1885 it was noted that 'the old-fashioned flue...is now rarely seen', and that the need was for 'a moderate heat, obtainable easily and at small cost, to tide over a bad time and save a nice little lot of plants from destruction'. For the many gardeners who did not require, or could not afford, 'elaborate arrangements' for heating by gas or hot water, Albion's oil stoves (December 5 1885, page 373) were found to 'answer completely for the saving of the floral pets during times of hard weather'. Toope's Patent Stoves (January 9 1886, page 433) were also recommended, particularly as they were said to produce no offensive smell or smoke. The 'cheerful' stoves of Wright & Butler (February 20 1886, page 514) produced light as well as heat, but 'it should be noted that when an escape for the products of combustion can be provided, it is all the better'.

A good barometer and thermometer was invaluable for judging when the weather was likely to make heating necessary, and Freeman & Freeman's model (Februry 7 1885, page 481) was 'a wonderfully cheap combination'. For gardeners of a more technical frame of mind, an electric thermometer with an alarm bell (February 24 1894, page 426), to warn of fire and frost, could be set up. It was suggested that two bells could be used, one to warn of high and the other of low temperatures. Many houses were already fitted with electric bells, but if one had to be bought, 'for alarm purposes, the smaller sized gongs are preferable because the tone is more shrill and piercing'. If more than one plant house was to be fitted with an alarm, a range of different sized bells would give a variety of tones to enable each particular house to be identified by sound. The alarm system was powered by a battery, which was very different to today's batteries. A Leclanché battery was recommended, but, the author tells us, Gassner, E.C.C., G.E.C., E.S., Hellesen, Edison-Lalande, Agglomerate Leclanché, Caporous Leclanché, and Fuller bichromate batteries could be used instead. The Leclanché batteries recommended needed to be kept in cool, dry conditions: 'a little rain water should be added occasionally to make up that lost by evaporation, and when the zinc rods show a white crust the outer cells should be washed out, the zincs cleaned, and a fresh, half-saturated solution of sal-ammoniac put in the clean cells'.

It would need to be a very keen gardener who would go to so much trouble to protect his plants, but for those who thought they could manage without heating in their plant houses, *Amateur Gardening* in 1886 reminded its readers of 'the dreadful winter of 1880...protracted far into March; and not only were tens of thousands of plants destroyed, but human life paid heavy penalties for its susceptibility to cold.' In 1881 the winter came late and extended into April, but 'since then we have had no real winter. We know nothing of the future, but experience teaches us to be always prepared against the worst.' A run of mild winters was obviously also a feature of life before global warming.

Those who did not want to heat the whole greenhouse, or who wanted to provide warmer conditions for a few special plants such as orchids, could make use of the Florists' Assistant (1894, page 464), designed to enclose a small area on the greenhouse staging. It was fitted with a charcoal purifier to absorb combustion fumes from oil or gas.

The summer, of course, presented different problems; temperatures needed to be kept down, and the sun's rays prevented from scorching delicate plants. Shading could be provided by Willesden blinds (May 1902 page xii) made to order from 'green, rot-proof scrim'.

Propagators and frames

Propagating plants from seed or cuttings could also be undertaken in the home, and was considered a particularly suitable occupation for invalids. The Toope's Plant Propagator (1886, page 491) was one of many designed for 'Parlour horticulture'. Heat could be provided by candles, oil or gas jets but when gas was used, care had to be taken to adjust the flame at dusk, when the gas companies increased the pressure.

Hot beds were in common use at the time, particularly in the gardens of larger houses. Fresh manure was covered with soil, which was gently warmed as the manure rotted, providing plants with bottom heat. A more convenient method of providing bottom heat was supplied by small propagators, often heated by kettles in which water was boiled once every twenty-four hours. The propagators were generally wooden boxes with glass tops, often raised on legs to a convenient working height (April 11 1885, page 589 and April 17 1886, page 612).For raising seeds there were glass seed covers (1887, page 636) supplied in nests of seven at 10s per nest.

The range of salads available in winter was limited, and watercress was a valuable crop to grow. Cuttings could be taken from any bunch of watercress. They were inserted in a pan of good soil plus a few lumps of chalk, stood in a water dish and covered with a glass bell jar (1884, page 430). In a warm place they rooted within a few days and supplied watercress for up to three months through the winter.

Frames and handlights were also popular for providing that little extra protection for slightly tender crops. 'Handlights' (March 13 1886, page 552) were similar to what we now call cloches. Cloches in those days were individual bell-shaped glass domes. Frames were useful for a wide range of crops, but those without a secure method of opening were not without their dangers, as C. J. Frazer's illustration (1886, page 516) shows. Frames with sliding glass lights (1885, page 516) were also available.

Frames could be heated simply and cheaply with an oil lamp (1884, page 311) as suggested by a reader in 1884. The metal box to hold the lamp was made from a preserved tongue tin.

There were fashions in flowers as in other areas, and auriculas had plenty of devotees. These perfect blooms, their flowers heavily marked with white or silver 'paste' were easily damaged by rain, and overwintering the plants was not easy. Enthusiasts could construct a special frame (September 1884, page 250) to enable their plants to receive just the right amount of air and moisture, with opening front and top lights, glass sides, and a special door in the wooden back to allow more thorough ventilation.

Fruit was always popular, but not just any fruit — the more exotic the better. While the larger houses grew grapes, pineapples and citrus fruits, even amateurs could try peaches, apricots and nectarines against a sheltered wall. Because they flowered early, the blossoms needed protection from cold late winter and early spring weather, and later the fruits could be damaged by heavy rain or hail. Gardeners could opt for a portable glass roof (1885, page 515) to keep off the worst of the weather or make more sure of success by enclosing the whole wall in glass (1886, page 537).

MESSENGER & CO.

Beg to call attention to their

IMPROVED HORTICULTURAL BUILDINGS

Which have won a world-wide repute or their great

EFFICIENCY, ELEGANCE, and ECONOMY.

Constructed so as to obtain, with the least obstruction to light and sun, the greatest strength and rigidity, at prices which, owing to unusual facilities, defy competition for first-class work. Gentlemen will do well to obtain an estimate from us before ordering elsewhere. Special attention given to Amateurs' Greenhouses, made in lights so as to be readily put up, and removed without taking out any glass. Illustrated Catalogues Free. Richly-Illustrated Catalogue, containng Hundreds of Illustrations of Winter Gardens, Conservatories, Vineries, &c., and all kinds of Greenhouse Fittings, Heating Apparatus, &c., for 24 stamps.

A GOLD MEDAL (the Highest Award) has been awarded to us in open competition for general excellence in Horticultural Buildings by the Society of Architects.

(1889)

MELON AND CUCUMBER FRAMES,

Glazed and painted, complete, 25s.

BEFORE Purchasing Greenhouses call and inspect stock at the Whittington Horticultural Works. Span-Roof Greenhouses from £5 5s. Lean-to from £4 14s. All kinds of Conservatories made to order. Catalogues free on application.—Note address.—GEO. DAWSON, Horticultural Builder, Highgate Hill, London, N.

(1885)

W. COOPER, Ltd.

AMATEUR SPAN-ROOF GREENHOUSE.

7 ft. by 3 ft., £2 16s.

For other sizes, see List.

(NOVEMBER 13 1897)

From 56/- From 18/-

COOPER'S GREENHOUSES!

ARE Without doubt the Cheapest, most complete, Simplest to erect, and best value for money in the Trade. It is a well-known fact that ordinary Builders could not Supply the Timber alone at the price which we Charge for a house Complete, with Staging, Ventilators, Glass, &c., &c., all ready for erecting by any Handy-man or Gardener. These Houses are made by Special Machinery, in lots of never less than one Hundred at the Time, and we are satisfied with small profits and quick returns.

We are NOW in a position to undertake extensions and repairs to any extent, and give estimates for alterations of, or additions to, existing Houses or Heating Apparatus. You would do well and will save 40 per cent. at least in buying from us. Under any circumstances do not place your orders for any kind of Horticultural Work until you have seen our Catalogue, which contains 364 pages and 1,200 illustrations, published at 1/-. But to all applicants during the next 14 days they will be

GIVEN AWAY.

Send at once. Mention "AMATEUR GARDENING,"

W. COOPER, Ltd., Horticultural Providers, 755, Old Kent Rd., London, S.E.

(OCTOBER 17 1896)

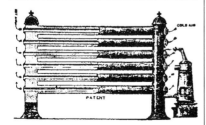

WINDOW CONSERVATORY, FURNISHED WITH PALMS AND DRACÆNAS.

(1885)

(DECEMBER 20 1884)

(NOVEMBER 1884)

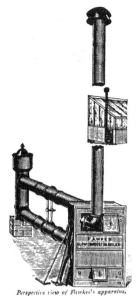

Perspective view of Fawkes's apparatus.

(JANUARY 16 1886)

No. 102.

(DECEMBER 5 1885)

(FEBRUARY 20 1886)

(JANUARY 1886)

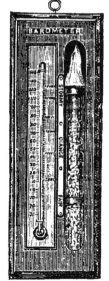

(FEBRUARY 7 1885)

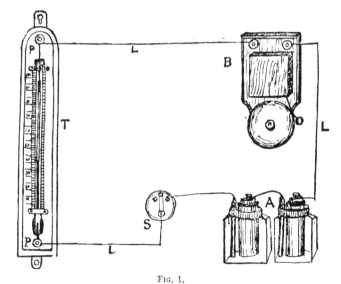

FIG. 1.

References.—A, Leclanché battery; B, electric bell; L, L, L, line wires; P, platinum connectors; S, switch; T, thermometer.

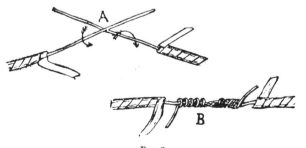

FIG. 2.

References.—A, ends of wires cleaned and crossed ready for making a joint; B, ends of wire twisted to form a joint.

(FEBRUARY 24 1894)

(APRIL 11 1885)

(1894)

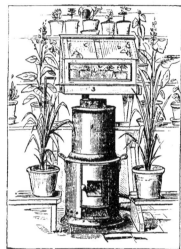

TOOPE'S PLANT PROPAGATOR.

(1886)

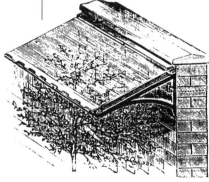

MODE OF STRIKING WATERCRESSES IN WINTER.

(1884)

(1885)

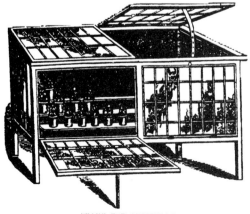

FRAME FOR AURICULAS.

(SEPTEMBER 1884)

"DARLINGTON" GLASS WALL COVER. (1886)

HORLEY'S NEW PATENT HAND LIGHTS,
THE "HANDY."

PATENT No. 13276—A.D. 1885.

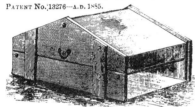

Size near 3 ft. long by 2 ft. wide, 9 in. glass sides, and 15 in. high to ridge (as engraving), 7s.   No. 2, 3 in. high at sides, and 9 in. high at ridge, 5s.

Illustrated Catalogue, 1d. Stamp.

M. E. HORLEY, Steam Horticultural Works,
TODDINGTON, BEDS.

(MARCH 13 1886)

C. J. FRAZER.
Horticultural Builder, Norwich.

The "Universal" Handlight Protectors.

For Kitchen Gardens, set of 6, covers 31 square feet, diminishing sizes, painted 3 coats and glazed with 21-oz. glass; per set, £2 12s.   Large stock ready for despatch.

Three-quarter Garden Frame, with (registered) set-opes, lights, 2 inches thick, glazed with 21-oz. glass, and painted 4 coats, 4 ft. by 6 ft.. £2 17s.; 8 ft. by 6 ft., £4 10s.; 12 ft. by 6 ft., £6 5s.   Cases, 6s.

THE CHEAPEST LEAN-TO FRAMES IN THE MARKET.

Glazed with 21-oz. glass, and painted 3 coats, fitted with strong joints and (registered) set-opes. 8 ft. by 4 ft., £2 2s.; 12 ft. by 4 ft., £2 15s.; 16 ft. by 4 ft., £3 10s.   Cases, 6s.

The illustration shows the largest of the set of six.

NEW "IMPROVED" HANDLIGHTS.

Made diminishing sizes, covers 17 square feet; painted three coats, and glazed with 21-oz. glass; per set, £2 7s. 6d.

Carriage paid to any Railway Station in England and Wales; also to Edinburgh, Glasgow, Dublin, and Belfast.

Illustrated Catalogues of Greenhouses and Frames, post free, two stamps.

See Advertisement alternate weeks.

(1886)

PLAN FOR HEATING A FRAME WITH A PARAFFIN LAMP.   (1884)

Fertilizers, composts and manures

It is sometimes surprising to discover how long products we think of as new have actually been available. In the 1990s gardeners have realized that peat is a limited resource and that we should be thinking of alternative bases for growing composts. Cocoa-fibre is one of the most promising alternatives, but it is hardly a new discovery. Over a hundred years ago cocoa-nut fibre was available by the sack load from a range of different suppliers (1885, page 480). There were many proprietary fertilizers, often with optimistic names — Daniels' Eureka Manure (November 1885, page 360) and Clay's Invigorator (March 15 1890, page 562) amongt them. As always, the manufacturers were not modest in their claims: 'all the elements necessary for the perfection of plant life...quick in action, lasting and economical. Suitable for every purpose where a manure is required.' With's Plant Food (August 13 1898, page vi) promised to 'act like magic', with a fairy on the bag to prove it. Clay's Fertiliser (1887, page 591) was a little more down to earth, with the explanation 'or plant food' in case anybody should not be quite clear what a fertilizer was.

Some fertilizers were a little more basic in origin: Pure Ichthemic Guano (fish dung) (1887, page 443) was 'useful everywhere...in flower garden, conservatory and greenhouse'. Then there was Canary Guano (1898, page ix) — not only 'the best in the world', but clean enough to be used by a lady. A lady was also pictured delicately forking in Wakeley's Hop Manure, a 'complete substitute for stable manure' (15 May 1915, page iv). Even before the motor car became really popular, good quality stable manure was apparently difficult to obtain. Wakeley's Hop Manure received an endorsement from the Royal Horticultural Society after its trial in the Society's gardens at Wisley.

Then there was the great scientific discovery for gardening — horticultural electricity. The manufacturers claimed amazing results for the use of Sun-Ray Magnets (1915 xxvi). 'The sparkling conductive metal alloy...attracts the ethereal electricity in somewhat the same way as the lightening conductor on a church spire, but with this vital difference. The lightning conductor conducts to earth the destructive electricity of the atmosphere, whereas the Sun-Ray magnets conduct its creative electricity'. The magnets were also claimed to prevent blight, wireworms and other destructive pests, as well as inducing tropical effects of growth, profusion of blooms, richness of colouring and a phenomenal increase of the flower's natural perfume. 'The thing seems almost too good to be true' the advertisement continues in a rare moment of honesty, 'yet the same disbelief existed when inventors introduced the telephone, the phonograph, wireless and flying machine'. Unlike these inventions, however, the Sun-Ray magnets have sadly not withstood the test of time.

Watering

The watering of plants and gardens, particularly before hoses were in common use, must have been a heavy and time-consuming job. The value of water would have been well appreciated, but water from commercial companies did not appear to have a very good reputation. The setting up of a complex system of tanks to collect rainwater from roofs was advised (January 24 1885, page 547). It was acknowledged that the initial rain washed down 'various materials' including soot, dead leaves and other rubbish that made the water unfit for household use, but as the rain continued, the roof was washed and 'a comparatively clear sample of rain water may be caught'. Tank A was fitted with a piece of sloping slate to prevent the water being stirred up as fresh rain water ran in. The initial dirty water then ran into tank C until it was full, when a ball valve sealed it off. 'Clean' water then filled tank A, from where it ran into tanks D and E, tank E being fitted with a filter across the centre. The water then drawn from tank E was used for laundry, cooking and making tea and coffee. 'There is no town water anywhere, by whatsoever company supplied, that can equal it for wholesomeness, brightness, and sweetness'. Which does not say a great deal for the quality of tap water at the time.

Much of the water for garden use was carried in swing water barrows (June 1 1889, page 60), which were wheeled from one part of the garden to another, a watering can being dipped into the barrow for filling. The barrows tipped forward so that they could be drained. Pushing a full barrow any distance cannot have been an easy task.

Watering cans do not seem to have been particularly easy to use, either. When the Haws can appeared in 1887 (May 21 1887, page 34) *Amateur Gardening* commented 'Any marked improvement on the old form of can so long in use deserves a passing word of commendation'. The new can was easy to fill, carry and use, and there was no danger of wetting one's feet. 'For lady amateurs this invention is a great boon.' Virtually identical cans are still available today — and from the same manufacturer.

Watering cans were fitted with roses to give a fine spray, but finer results could be achieved with a syringe. These, too, had their drawbacks: a thorough soaking appeared to be an inevitable accompaniment to any kind of watering. Dawkins Patent Watertight Plunger Syringe (1894, page 146) claimed to be a vast improvement over all other syringes — though in August 1894 they were compelled to offer their 'large surplus stock (doubtless due to the wet season) at half price'. The Cheltenham Garden Syringe (July 11 1896, page vi) claimed to cover a large area with a fine spray, the 5ft of suction hose 'preventing any stooping by the user'. The Patent Automatic Sprayer (1902, page viii) came nearer to modern pressure sprayers, the tank being filled and pumped up to deliver a jet from 40ft upwards. As well as garden use, the sprayer was recommended for washing windows and extinguishing small fires. Pumps such as the "Model" Garden Engine (1902, page 174) and Heathman's Iron Lift Pump (1889, page 484) were also used. Heathman also supplied the fearsome-sounding hydropult. The 'indispensable' Watering Machine (June 15 1912, page ix) consisted of an oak barrel on an iron frame, and was claimed to throw water to a distance of 60ft.

Hoses made from gutta-percha or rubber were introduced around the middle of the nineteenth century, and became increasingly popular as a quick and easy way of supplying water to large areas of the garden. Merryweather hoses (August 1887, page iv) were used by 'Colonial Offices, Indian Governments, Crown Agents for the Colonies, Crystal Palace, Metropolitan Board of Works and all the gardeners of the nobility and gentry'. The company supplied both armoured Sphincter Grip and unarmoured Non-kinkable Red Grey Hose (May 1891 page 30). For watering lawns and large areas, the Merryweather Portable Lawn Fountain (4 September 1886, page iv) was a revolving sprinkler powered by water pressure, which by 1891 was being advertised 'as supplied to H.R.H. the Prince of Wales'. Merryweathers should have known about hoses and water supply: they were also manufacturers of fire engines.

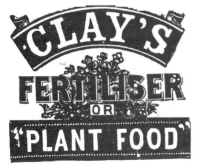

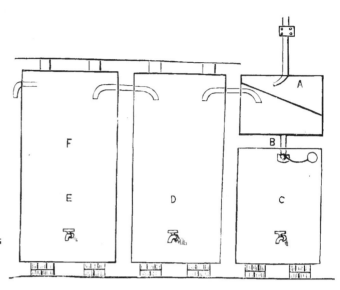

(MAY 15 1915)

Pests and diseases

A major concern of gardeners has always been — and is always likely to be — controlling the large number of pests and diseases that spoil plants. One of the commonest and most effective remedies was tobacco, and nicotine continued to be used as an effective insecticide for many years before it was finally banned because of its dangerous properties. The Patent Fumigator of 1884 (May 31 1884, page 49) was 'designed particularly to enable ladies, and those to whom the smoking of a tobacco pipe would be unpleasant, to free their plants from greenfly...with comfort and convenience'. Smouldering tobacco in a chamber was kept alight by pressing the 'puff ball' with the thumb: the fumes could then be directed at plants through the pipe. Brinkman's Fumigator (1896, page viii) used 'pipe refuse and cigar ends' but despite this was advertised as suitable for use by ladies. Tobacco was also available in powder form, which could be applied through Binko's Patent Powder Distributor (June 12 1886, page): this 'useful article' cost one shilling. The Duplex Powder Distributor and Dredging Box (August 13 1887, page 178) had the advantage of being capable of applying liquids as well as powders, with a choice of nozzles.

By 1893 there was a range of fumigating materials that did not need any equipment for their application, and demand for fumigators had fallen. This did not stop the Goode Fumigating Company from introducing 'one of the most perfect fumigators of its kind that we have ever seen'(January 27 1894, supplement page). The fumigator contained a clockwork rotary fan to ensure the rapid and complete burning of tobacco papers, and a gap between the inner and outer casing allowed cool air to mix with the smoke as it was delivered from the nozzle. Once wound up, the fan would run for 15 minutes, enabling the fumigator to be left unattended to fill the greenhouse with smoke 'thus avoiding the unpleasantness attendant on the use of other apparatus'. The only drawback *Amateur Gardening* could see was its high price — half a guinea.

Among the new products that were replacing the old-fashioned tobacco papers were the Lethorion vapour cone (1888, page 468), McDougall's Insecticide Fumer (March 12 1897, page xii) and Campbell's Fumigating Insecticide (1891, page 44).

For applying liquids, the Alpha Sprayer (May 4 1912, page 17) was pressurized by a foot pump 'exactly as a cycle tyre is inflated'. For larger areas, Boulton & Paul's spraying machine (May 13 1912, page xix) contained 'an automatic arrangement for keeping insecticide preparations well mixed during use' but for most amateur gardeners the 3s Beanco sprayer (22 May 1915, page xix) was sufficient. 'Maximum efficiency with minimum labour' was the boast of the Belmite self-acting powder blower (1915, page 79).

There were plenty of insecticides available, many of them making a feature of being non-poisonous. Hughes Aphicide (April 24 1885, page 624) employed a novel method of application which enabled the insecticide to be applied to the underside of the leaves. Firtree Oil was claimed to kill all insects and parasites as well as mildew and blight, while Tropical Beetle Powder destroyed 'beetles, cockroaches, cricket bugs, fleas, mosquitoes...in greenhouses, for animals, and bed clothing'.

Katakilla Wash (May 4 1912, page 17) was free from 'nicotine, arsenic, copper or other dangerous poison' but still killed 'practically all garden insect pests'. Rosika Insecticide (September 1891, page 214), Cirengol (June 22 1907, page 103) and Vaporite (1908, page 649) were 'effective and harmless' and 'reliable and non-poisonous' but if you wanted to save money you could make your own insecticide from Compo soap (May 1915, page 31) — 10 gallons for 2d, though this presumably didn't include the cost of the paraffin or methylated spirits that had to be added.

Weeding has always been one of the less popular gardening chores, and advertisements for weedkillers made much of their labour-saving aspects. Acme Weedkiller (May 1891, page 30) was said to save 'more than twice its cost in labour' while Sandwith's weary gardener on his knees (1898, page xii) must have struck an immediate chord with all gardeners. Eureka Weedkiller (1912, page xvii) saved 'weary weeding and laborious rolling'.

Not all pests were dealt with by chemical means. Some accuracy would have been needed to use the 'no noise, no ammunition' Wasp and Fly Gun (May 13 1912, page 57) effectively but if you preferred something nearer the real thing, Timmins guns, an adaptation of the catapult (November 1891, page 302), were 'perfectly silent, portable, durable...will kill rabbits'. Wire netting (November 1885, page 444) was one reasonably sure way of keeping rabbits at bay and could also be shaped into pea guards to protect the seedlings (March 13 1885, page 550).

If birds were your problem, the musical scarecrow (1884, page 167) was 'warranted to terrify all the birds in the district'. A puff of wind blowing on the bat fixed to the left arm kept the figure turning while the stick on the right arm rung the bell at each turn. The scarecrow could be made at home from a wooden frame and a Guy Fawkes mask.

Seeds and other items to be stored were at risk from rats and mice: even when suspended from a hanging beam they were apparently not safe. This 'checkmate to rats and mice that have learnt to perform on the tight-rope' (1884, page 299) involved threading loosely fitted discs of cardboard or tin on the rope or wire, so that when the animals tried to climb over them the discs would spin round and throw them off. (1884 page 299).

Earwigs could be captured in matchboxes left slightly open and suspended on a wire hook near the blooms of susceptible plants (1893, page 192); the author recommends the small-sized safety match-boxes as preferable to the phosphorus-tipped type. Cats can be a problem scratching up seedbeds, and a rather drastic-looking solution was dreamt up by an *Amateur Gardening* reader in 1889 (page 183). Using 'the waste cuttings from a tinman's shop' and a pair of tinman's shears, narrow strips of tin were cut at an angle to ensure a sharply pointed end, then soldered on to a flat piece of metal to form crosses. The ends of the strips were turned up, and the whole thing lightly covered with soil wherever troublesome cats frequented. Cats, not surprisingly, were said to beat a hasty retreat as soon as their feet came into contact with the 'sharp, barb-like points'.

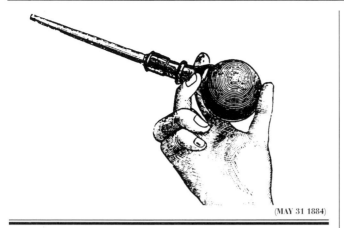

(MAY 31 1884)

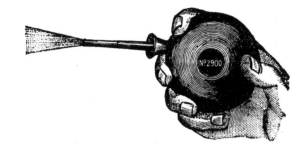

(JUNE 12 1886)

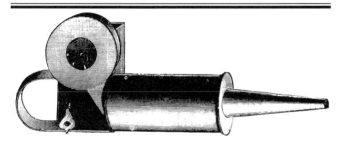

(JANUARY 27 1894)

(AUGUST 13 1887)

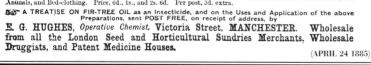

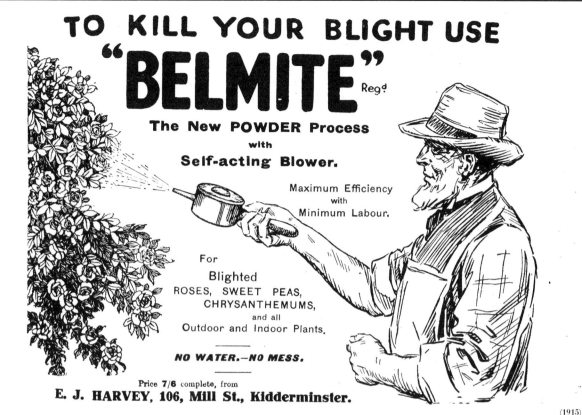
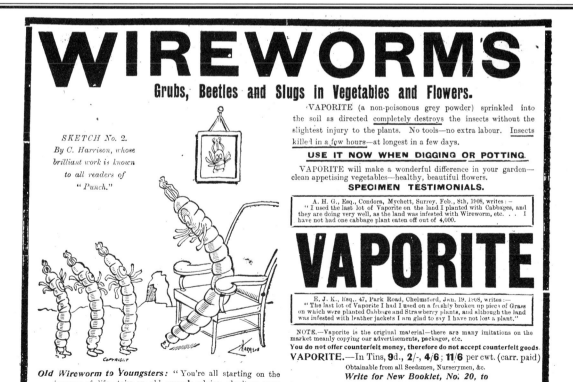

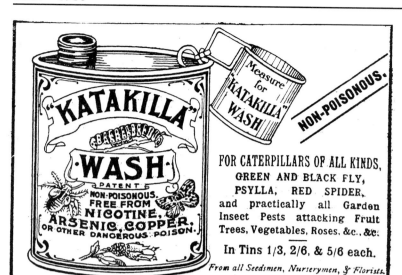
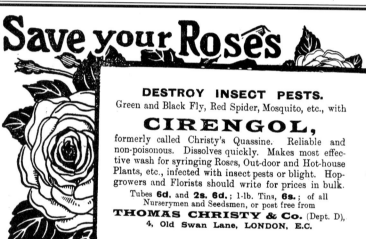

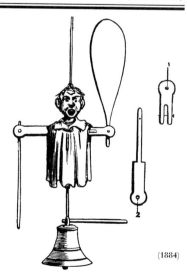

THE EARWIG TRAP.

(1893)

Patent No. 17,660. Dec. 1, 1888.

E. P. TIMMINS, Patentee, 90 Balsall Heath Road, **BIRMINGHAM**.

These GUNS are an adaptation of the Catapult. They are perfectly silent, portable, durable, shoot accurately, use shot or bullet, will kill rabbits. Effective range, 40 yards. 5s. 6d., 10s. 6d., and 16s., post free. Liberal trade terms.

(NOVEMBER 1891)

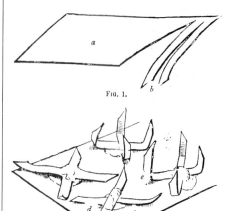

FIG. 1.

FIG. 2.
ANTI-CAT CONTRIVANCE.

(1889)

A CHECKMATE TO RATS AND MICE.

(1884)

Miscellaneous inventions

There was hardly a week in which a whole clutch of new inventions did not appear in *Amateur Gardening*, for there was a great interest in novelties of all sorts. Inventor and amateur horticulturist James Crute developed Crute's Concave Flower Pot (July 12 1884, page 121) 'a common, old-fashioned pot ...brought to mechanical perfection by a few ingenious touches'. The concave base, with drainage holes in the centre and at the sides, drained freely while being 'absolutely proof against the entrance of worms'. The fact that the pots were more expensive than the ordinary type prevented them being widely taken up, but Mr Crute went on to produce a variety of decorative garden pottery (July 31 1886, page 162).

Decoration was required indoors, too, and plain pots were felt to be unartistic and unsightly. 'Majolica and other fancy pottery' were too expensive for everyday use, however, particularly while 'careless maids exist'. Pot covers manufactured from Thetford Patent Pulp (1894, page 92) were ideal for careless maids, being practically unbreakable. The rustic designs were thought to be 'exceedingly pretty and effective in appearance ... astonishingly low in price'. Sankey's Garden Pots (April 26 1890, page viii) were plain but of 'beautiful colour, and symmetrical in appearance, well finished'. When a plant began to outgrow its pot, the New Plant Collar (1889 page 203) extended the rooting space without repotting. It was made or terracotta-coloured metal, and could be extended to fit any size pot.

For displaying trailing plants in the home, the Self-adjusting Flower Pot Suspender (1891, page 9) was found to be 'light and elegant in appearance, and far superior to the wire baskets formerly used'. In the garden, Royal Doulton's Terra Cotta Vases (1907, page 13) were of a classic design that has persisted to the present day. The ornate trellis-bottomed window box (July 12 1891, page 113) was not only more elegant than the normal, straight-sided boxes, but contained trellis-work in the base to allow for drainage while holding the soil in place, and a zinc lining to protect the box from rotting.

The principal of the Island (June 15 1895, page 76) was to protect pot plants from attack by slugs, earwigs and other pests by surrounding them with a moat. The earthenware saucer was kept filled with water, while the pot stood clear of the water on a raised central section. Other inventions that appeared at the time were the Beckett Cup and Tube (1894, page 256), a device for securing and exhibiting show chrysanthemums, and a glazing bar for glazing greenhouses without putty (April 21 1888, page 608), a 'more modern and satisfactory method' of glazing. Improvements in greenhouse construction had, in 1888, placed owning a greenhouse 'within the reach of all who can afford a five pound note'. Wood had largely been replaced by metal, leading to greenhouses which were 'lighter, more durable, and better adapted to the system of dry glazing which is now so much in vogue'.

Ladders were essential for attending to wall-trained fruit trees, and telescopic ladders and steps were particularly useful. The popularity of tennis lead to a call for 'umpire's step chairs', too (1889 page 132).

There has always been a need for long-lasting plant labels: Acme Plant Labels (March 7 1885, page 529) were said to be imperishable 'for all practical purposes'; they were sold at 12s to 18s per gross, 'a price that astonishes one by its smallness as compared with the perfection of the article'.

The setback given to seedlings by transplanting could be overcome by using T. P. Seed Raisers (1915, page 587). Seeds were sown directly into compost in the seed raisers, which had largely rotted when it was time to transplant, and could be peeled off with no root disturbance to the plant.

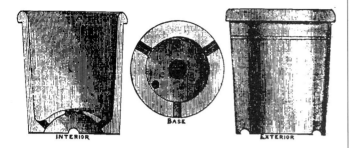

(JULY 12 1884)

(1894)

(1889)

of deportment the palm must be awarded to the Veratrums, which, although perfectly hardy, require the shelter of glass to prevent the wind and rain tearing their large handsome leaves into ribbons. *V. album* and *V. nigrum* are sufficiently distinct to allow of their being grown in the same collection. The hardy Yuccas, but with one exception, are rather too coarse for

CRUTE'S PATENT GARDEN POTTERY.

AT the great Liverpool Exhibition of the Royal Horticultural Society, a silver medal was awarded to Mr. James Crute, of 14, Knight-rider Street, London, E.C., for an interesting

are not so well adapted, because of necessity they cost a trifle more than the common pots.

Having achieved a triumph thus far, Mr. Crute has applied his principle in the production of flower-boxes, vases, urns, and other decorative examples of garden pottery. In this department he has been singularly successful, more especially

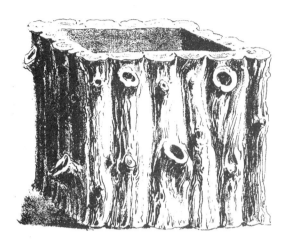

cultivation under glass, and the exception is *Y. filamentosa variegata*, which is certainly a most beautiful plant in its peculiar style of growth.

The cultivation of the whole of the subjects here named can be dismissed in a few words, as they all grow freely in a compost consisting of sound turfy loam, mixed with a small proportion of leaf-mould, peat, and silver-sand.

display of garden pottery, of a quite ingenious construction, and in a beautiful and novel style and material. Mr. Crute applies his principle to the common garden-pot, or to the highly finished classic urn or vase, and it consists in forming the bottom of the pot concave like the bottom of a wine bottle. This concave bottom is pierced with holes and covered (inside) with a loose,

in the colour of the material. We present a few figures selected from the many examples of Mr. Crute's manufacture, as these will be more useful than mere descriptions. We are bound to add, however, that the colours are imitative of stone, bark, and other materials that might be used in such a manufacture; and being burnt in, and the ware being of singular hardness, per-

FRANCOA APPENDICULATA.

IN our issue of July 10, 1886, we dealt with the Francoas, and recommended amongst others *F. appendiculata* for the garden. We now present a figure of this beautiful plant, which is bold, and of distinct character. It is robust in habit, and the flowers are of a rosy hue.

perforated tile made for the purpose, the use of which saves all the trouble of "crocking," and ensures at once perfect drainage, and the exclusion of worms. The common pots made on this principle prove to be of special value in the cultivation of specimen plants, and are likely to be much used by cultivators for high-class work, but for rough work and for market growers they

manency is secured with the additional qualification of a power to resist extreme conditions of weather.

DOUBLE-FLOWERED CAMOMILE, *Anthemis nobilis flore pleno*, is an evergreen growing about one foot in height. The flowers are white, and appear in August. It is often called the white bachelor's buttons.

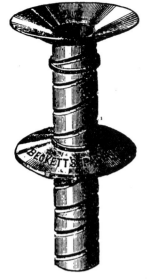

(1894)

(JULY 12 1891)

(JUNE 15 1895)

Telescopic Ladders.
Telescopic Steps.
Telescopic Trestles.
Convertible Ladder Steps.
Universal Step Ladders.
Turnover Step Ladders.
Folding Pole Ladders.
Lattice Steps, very Light.
Umpire's Step Chairs.

Great variety of Designs and Sizes. Sizes 5 ft. to 60 ft.

ORDER DIRECT, CARRIAGE PAID.
PRICE LISTS FREE.

HEATHMAN & CO.,
2, ENDELL STREET,
AND
11, HIGH STREET,
LONDON, W.C.

(1889)

Acme Plant Labels as manufactured by Mr. John Pinches, 27, Oxendon Street, Coventry Street, London, are the very best ready made labels for general purposes that have been hitherto offered. The subjoined diagrams accurately represent them, but they have qualities that no diagram can show. They are made of hard metal with raised white letters on a black ground; the inscription therefore cannot be washed out or rubbed out, and for all practical purposes they may be described as imperishable. The labels here figured are sold at 12s. to 18s. per gross; a price that astonishes one by its smallness as compared with the perfection of the article.

(MARCH 7 1885)

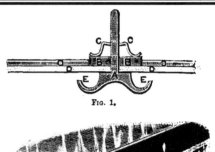

FIG. 1.

(1891)

SIDE VIEW   FIG. 2.   (APRIL 21 1888)

Gardeners' clothing

Keen gardeners are never put off by bad weather, but they do need appropriate clothing. The Cravenette waterproofing process (May 7 1892, page 11) rendered clothes 'porous and healthy', though the advertisement makes no claims for their being waterproof in anything more than 'a slight shower'. Footwear was very important in the nineteenth and early twentieth century: this was well before the days of the rubber wellington boot. The Gardener's Boot (December 15,1897 page viii) protected its wearer from damp feet: the advertisement included a rather irrelevant diagram of a foot with a somewhat oddly positioned 'joint' and a clearly labelled 'leg' just in case anyone should be in any doubt about its identity. Regal shoes (1912, page xvii) did not look particularly appropriate for gardening, but claimed to ensure a perfect fit, being made 'on anatomical models'. They were not only available in five widths, but were supplied in quarter sizes. More practical for wet weather gardening were grained leather clogs from the Garden Boot Warehouse (1907, page 274): a snip at 3/6 delivered to the door.

Lady gardeners would have appreciated waterproof Gauntlet gloves (June 4 1898, page x), which not only kept hands clean and dry, but prevented dress sleeves 'from being soiled whilst gardening'. Sleeves could also be protected by Jap-rush Gauntlet Cuffs (1912, page xviii). They were available in three sizes: maid's, woman's and men's. A good hat was also a necessity for the smart gardener: John Piggot advertised 'every kind of hat for garden wear' (July 13 1912, page iii).

Garden furniture

For ladies who did not wish to wear a hat, shade from the sun could be provided by the Baldwin Attachments (1891, page 123), a stand and clamp to fix a sunshade in any position. Sitting out in the garden was an enjoyable pastime, and there were plenty of benches and chairs on offer. Andrew Potter offers a chair complete with a fixed parasol (1895, page 442), while folding garden chairs were for sale at the 'ridiculously low figure' of 3s each (May 16 1896, page x). Complete weather protection could be provided by the Eden Tent (1898 page viii), a 'work of art' with no centre pole to get in the way.

Enjoying the pleasures of the garden must have waned a little during the First World War; there was more hard work to be done, and less time for sitting in the sun. The furniture and building manufacturers W. Cooper begged 'a little consideration from our clients who have orders on hand' when the whole works was commandeered by the War Office (20 June 1915, page vi).Walter Todd (24 July 1915, page v), on the other hand, found himself making special bargains of rustic arches, seats and other garden furniture in order to clear surplus stocks.

You need not stop work for a slight Shower if you wear Garments WATERPROOFED by the

POROUS and HEALTHY!

(MAY 7 1892)

(1891)

WAR! WAR! WAR!

I AM PREPARED, during the present WAR PERIOD, to make EXCEPTIONAL SACRIFICES, and am offering many SPECIAL BARGAINS of SURPLUS STOCKS of Rustic Arches, Seats, and other Garden Furniture, at prices within the reach of EVERY AMATEUR GARDENER.

REMEMBER, the Goods I manufacture are of THE BEST QUALITY.

EVERY ARTICLE is Substantially Made by Practical Men.

A glimpse of one corner of my works.

SEND for YOUR COPY of my "1915 SUMMER CLEARANCE SHEET." Post free on application.

WALTER TODD, "Suit-all" Rustic Factory, Smethwick, Staffs.

(JULY 24 1915)

No More SOILED or TORN SLEEVES.

6d PER PAIR POST FREE. WONDERFUL VALUE.

JAP-RUSH GAUNTLET CUFFS are all the rage. For garden or house wear. Waist for a pair now. Selling in thousands. Light, Durable, Washable, Made in three sizes, Maid's, Woman's and Men's. Orders sent in rotation. Price 6d. per pair (Postals preferred) post paid anywhere. Only address:

FRANKS & CO., Dept. 11, 55 the Side, Newcastle-on-Tyne,

(1912)

JOHN PIGGOTT, LTD.

EVERY KIND OF HAT FOR GARDEN WEAR.

Send for Sale List.

REAL FOLDING PANAMAS.—Wonderful Value in Panamas, the lightest, coolest, and most comfortable hat to wear. Special Sale Price, 4 11. Worth 7 each. Postage 4d.

"EVERYTHING" FOR THE GARDEN at this ADDRESS

117-118, Cheapside & Milk St, London, E.C.

(JULY 13 1912)

ANDREW POTTER. LONDON WORKS. READING.

ILLUSTRATED PRICE LIST OF ABOVE GOODS AND ALL OTHER KINDS OF GARDEN REQUISITES FREE.

MAKER TO H.M. THE QUEEN & H.R.H. THE PRINCE OF WALES.

PLEASE NAME PAPER.

(1895)

REGAL SHOES 16/6 & 21/-

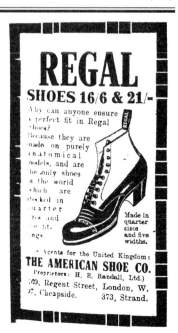

Why can anyone ensure a perfect fit in Regal Shoes? Because they are made on purely anatomical models, and are the only shoes in the world which are stocked in quarter sizes and five fittings.

Made in quarter sizes and five widths.

Agents for the United Kingdom: THE AMERICAN SHOE CO. (Proprietors: H. E. Randall, Ltd.) 109, Regent Street, London, W. 27, Cheapside. 373, Strand.

(1912)

Medicines and other aids

Gardeners were helped in their hobby by quite a range of medical preparations and sustaining drinks. One of the most frequently advertised was Beecham's Pills – 'worth a guinea a box'.

Unfettered by trading standards legislation, the pills were claimed to be useful for 'bilious and nervous disorders ... sick headache, giddiness, fulness, and swelling after meals, dizziness and drowsiness, cold chills, flushings of heat, loss of appetite, shortness of breath, costiveness, scurvy, blotches on the skin, disturbed sleep, frightful dreams, and all nervous and trembling sensations', giving relief in twenty minutes. Beecham's Magic Cough Pills were no less miraculous (1884, page 552). Calvert's Carbolic Ointment also had a wide application – 'piles, scalds, cuts, chilblains, sore eyes, sunburn, earache, rheumatic pains, throat colds and skin ailments' (1893, page 33). Sambuline ointment relieved irritation from insect bites, heat and 'chafing through exertion or exposure to the sun at gardening' (1907, page 54) Surprisingly little reference was made to the First World War in *Amateur Gardening*, but readers were frequently exhorted to send Pears soap to 'the boys at the Front' (1914 June 12, page xiv).

Perhaps gardening was felt to be a suitable pastime for invalids, who would benefit from Benger's Food – 'retained when all other foods are rejected' (1895, page 466). Or possibly coffee was a more pleasant restorative; made 'in a few seconds' with Symington's Coffee Essences (1892, page 48). Mason's Beer could be drunk with a clear conscience: not only was it non-intoxicating, it was 'health-giving and invigorating ... and deals a decisive blow at the lassitude inseparable from sultry weather' (1897, page 50 x) Dr. Tibble's Vi-Cocoa was not just a pleasant drink, either; a gardener from Bromley claimed to have been 'a different man' since substituting this brand of cocoa for tea (1902, page 314). And if all else failed, you could always turn to Wolfe's Schnapps, the 'good old drink of the healthy Dutch people'. This, too, possessed 'medicinal properties of supreme value'.

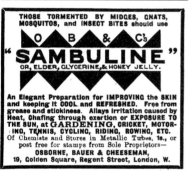

1919–1930

The years between the two World Wars brought mixed fortunes for the people of the British Isles. Peace did not bring immediate prosperity; unemployment was high, though the average weekly wage for an unskilled workman, at £4, had quadrupled since before the Great War. Improving economic conditions and a reaction against the grim years of war brought the gaiety and frivolity for which the Twenties are famous, but the same period saw the General Strike, followed within a few years by a disastrous economic slump.

As the thirties approached, fewer servants were employed, and fewer gardeners: increasingly, houseowners were undertaking their own gardening. In 1926 the Royal Horticultural Society's amateur show included classes for 'those amateurs whose average garden wage-bill does not exceed £4 a week' and 'those amateurs who employ no gardener' (1926, page 15).

Garden tools

The needs of all gardeners remained much the same. Plenty of tools and equipment were available to them: businesses such as that of T. Bath & Co. (14 May 1921, page 29) stocked a wide range that included bungalows, at £45, and motor-cycle and side-car houses among the lawn mowers, garden rollers and greenhouse heaters. Poultry keeping was also popular, with brooders, incubators, poultry runs and grit crushers among the equipment on offer.

The war had helped women to gain their emancipation, and though the woman appearing in Richard Melhuish's advert (March 18 1923, page 732) does not look very practically dressed for lawn mowing, at least she is doing the job . It is also a woman who is using the lawn edge trimmer from Thomas Gunn (1926, page 75). Despite being described as 'light' this complex-looking implement looks as though it would have been particularly awkward in use. The Star lawn edge clipper featured the following year (1927, page 919) appears to be a great deal easier. An idea of the turmoil in the economic situation of the country can be gained by comparing prices between Gunns adverts of 1924 and 1927: in 1924 their Success barrow (February 23, page 869) cost 33/9 while three years later the price had come down to 29/6. Pruners and garden rollers were also cheaper.

Soil cultivation has always been one of the most arduous aspects of gardening, and there have always been tools that claim to make the job simple. Gunn's Planet Junior (February 23 1924, page 869) combined hoe, cultivator and plough 'conditions the soil with ease and speed' and was 'capable of almost any kind of garden work'. Their Andyo undertook ridging, hoeing and culti-vating, while the Success Patent Digger 'transforms labour into pleasant exercise'.

The Cuma combined hand plough and cultivator (May 7 1921, page xix) was similar to the Planet Junior and was claimed to do 'more work in a day than can be done with a spade in a week'. Combined tools were quite popular: the Trinity rake (18 June 1921, page vii) was a combined hoe, rake and grubber, saving 'time, labour and money'. More traditional tools — a rake, a vari-ety of hoes and a fork — were contained in the Newman Gardening Kit, (11 March 1922, page xxv) but what made these 'something absolutely new' was the fact that they were supplied with one handle to fit all the tools.

The H.S.Tiller (April 5 1924, page 1018) was used to pro-duce a finely broken down surface soil for seedbeds, but the Warwick Tiller not only prepared seedbeds, stated the manufactur-ers, it also took the place of fork, rake and hoe.

More commonplace garden tools were not so widely advertised, but Spear & Jackson's Neverbend spade (1921 Page 423) — 'the greatest improvement in Garden Tools since steel superseded iron' — was said to be lighter in weight while still tougher than competitors.

Labour saving was a major claim of lawn-mower manufacturers, too. The novelty of these machines, which were originally thought to provide pleasant and healthy exercise, had worn off, and lawn mowing had become a chore. The J. P. Mower (1923, page 798) took 'the "O" out of mowing'; it was easy to adjust and ran 'like a Rolls-Royce'. Speedwell mowers (1926, page 58) made the whole operation child's play , and the Premier (1927, page 1000) mowed 'without effort. So easy running a child can use it.' If you didn't have a child, you could still get the job done by horse, pony or donkey — or buy a Ransomes' motor mower (May 14 1921, page 27). There was still a place for hand-operated shears, though, where the mower could not reach: Gunn's shears (1926, page 135) were fitted with rollers to take the weight off the operator's arms, and their long handles meant they could be used in a standing position. Once the war was over, Wilkinson Sword (March 18 1922, page 721) began to turn away from the manufacture of swords and bayonets to produce pruners, among other products. Their pruners looked very similar to today's secateurs — though the Barrows pruner of 1921 (May 14, page 27) appears rather more complicated — and Wilkinson Sword's Plucca pruner also doubled up as fruit and flower gatherer as it held the cut stems.

SAMPLES of our BARGAINS during our GREAT
Final Clearance Sale
25 to 75% Reductions off usual list prices.
EVERY ARTICLE IS NEW, PERFECT AND COMPLETE AS LIST.
WHEN ONCE CLEARED CANNOT BE REPEATED AT THE PRICE.

SEND FOR FINAL SALE CATALOGUE No. 4, POST FREE.

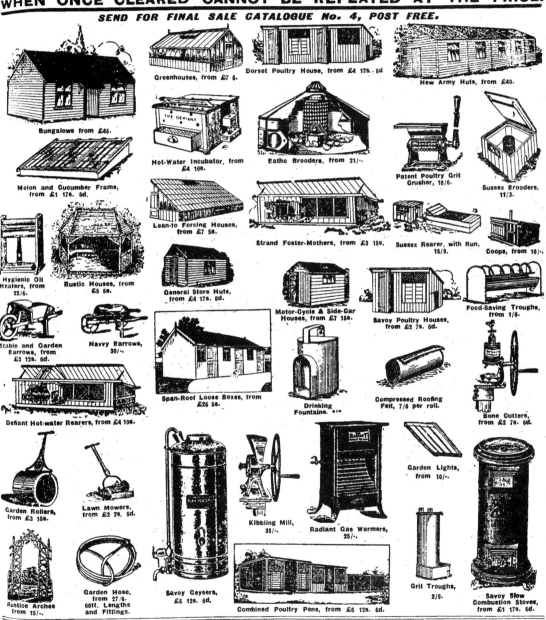

Greenhouses, from £7 5.

Dorset Poultry House, from £4 12s. 6d.

New Army Huts, from £40.

Bungalows from £45.

Hot-Water Incubator, from £4 10s.

Batho Brooders, from 21/-.

Patent Poultry Grit Crusher, 16/6.

Sussex Brooders, 11/3.

Melon and Cucumber Frame, from £1 17s. 6d.

Lean-to Forcing Houses, from £7 5s.

Strand Foster-Mothers, from £3 15s.

Sussex Rearer, with Run, 18/9.

Coops, from 10/-.

Hygienic Oil Heaters, from 22/6.

Rustic Houses, from £5 5s.

General Store Huts, from £4 17s. 6d.

Motor-Cycle & Side-Car Houses, from £7 15s.

Savoy Poultry Houses, from £2 7s. 6d.

Food-Saving Troughs, from 1/6.

Stable and Garden Barrows, from £2 12s. 6d.

Navvy Barrows, 30/-.

Span-Roof Loose Boxes, from £26 5s.

Drinking Fountains.

Compressed Roofing Felt, 7/6 per roll.

Bone Cutters, from £2 7s. 6d.

Defiant Hot-water Rearers, from £4 10s.

Garden Rollers, from £3 15s.

Lawn Mowers, from £2 2s. 6d.

Kibbling Mill, 35/-.

Radiant Gas Warmers, 25/-.

Garden Lights, from 10/-.

Savoy Geysers, £5 12s. 6d.

Grit Troughs, 2/9.

Savoy Slow Combustion Stoves, from £1 17s. 6d.

Rustic Arches from 15/-.

Garden Hose, from 27/6. 60ft. Lengths and Fittings.

Combined Poultry Pens, from £6 12s. 6d.

All Orders carefully packed on rail at Works. Our new Show Rooms are now Open, where samples of the various goods can be seen. Greenhouses, Poultry Appliances, Rustic Work, Huts, &c., all erected. Also sections of the larger Wooden Buildings.

T. BATH & CO., LTD., 18, Savoy St., London, W.C.2.
Telephone: GERRARD 5797.

(MAY 1921)

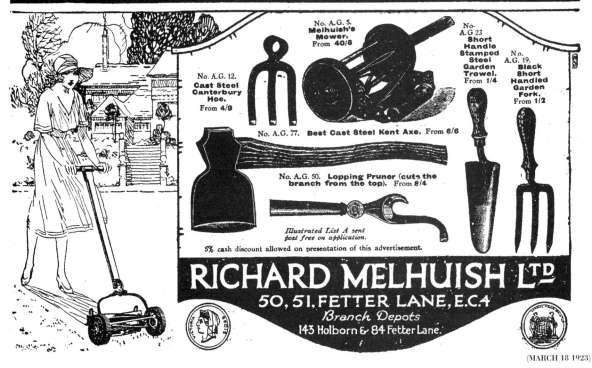
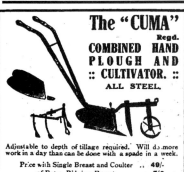

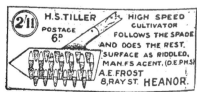

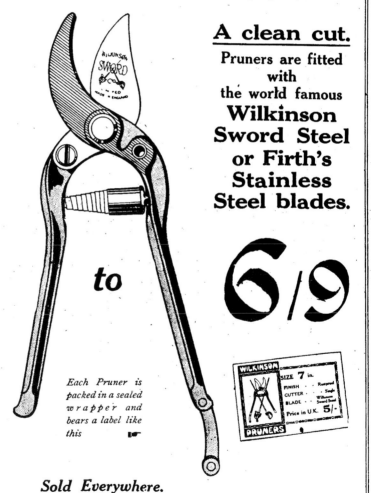

Greenhouses and frames

While some greenhouses of the period still retained something of the ornate Victorian style, (1923, page 69) most began to be more practical. Smaller gardens were becoming important, as Boulton & Paul's advert shows (November 10 1923, page 550), though by today's standards this is still a moderately large greenhouse at 10ft by 8ft. It would have been interesting to see whether their claim that the greenhouse could be erected by unskilled labour in 90 minutes stood up in reality!

If there was no room or money for a full-size greenhouse, the Letchworth Wall Frame (1923, page 589) provided a 'bijou hothouse' where one could 'grow flowers all winter for 11/2d a day' — the same cost as heating the Woodworkers Propagator Frame (May 12 1923, page 44). This frame had three compartments heated to different temperatures, so that seedlings and young plants could be gradually hardened off before planting out. The propagator did away with the need for 'the objectionable practice of making up a hot bed of stable manure.'

For large and small gardens, there were Chase Continuous Cloches (February 9 1924, page 817) to protect plants and ensure early crops. Both the simple, two-piece tent pattern and the large barn cloche were available, as well as alpine plant protectors.

Pests and diseases

Between the wars, trying to avoid the ravages of plant pests and diseases occupied the gardener just as much as in any other age. Manufacturers were under no obligation to reveal the ingredients of their products, so gardeners had to rely on the claims made in the advertisements. Katakilla (1923, page 65) 'contains the most powerful Insect Killer ever discovered', but apart from the fact that it is not nicotine or 'other poisons', the manufacturers give no further hints as to its identity. However, it was the 'sole property of McDougall's' so gardeners were led to believe it was unique.

Claims for pesticides were still wide-ranging. Sanitas Powder (1923 page 41) was said to be useful against 'slugs, worms and all other garden pests...effective in the extreme'. Interestingly, it is one of the few products that does not make a point of its non-poisonous nature. Solomia (May 26 1923, page 94) was 'harmless to all save insect pests and fungoid growths', a non-poisonous spray that 'really kills'. Abol (June 2 1923, page 115) and Ferry Brand (1926, page 157) insecticides were also said to kill both pests and diseases while being 'clean and wholesome to handle', 'non poisonous'— and even not damaging to paintwork.

Prevention is generally better than cure, and strawing down of strawberries helps protect them against damp, soil splashes and slugs. Loose straw is not the easiest of materials to handle, though, and Magna Strawmats (1926, page 971) did much the same job while being simpler and tidier in use. These were the forerunners of modern fibre strawberry mats which have now largely been replaced by black polythene.

Rodents were responsible for much damage to young plants, seeds and stored crops, and rats were common near many homes. Traps and poisons, ferrets and terriers were used to control them, but Liverpool virus (November 19 1921, page xviii) was said to be far more effective than any of these, killing not only the rats that ate the bait, but those that came into contact with them afterwards. This rather unpleasant-sounding germ warfare was held to be 'harmless to humans, poultry, farm and domestic animals'.

EVERY GARDENER USES **"KATAKILLA"**

FOR
SPRAYING

"AS EASY AS IT LOOKS."

FRUIT
FLOWERS
VEGETABLES

Sudden death to Green Fly, Caterpillars and other Pests.

In Powder form, ready for mixing with water.
No danger of leakage and loss.

Non-Poisonous. Non-Corrosive.

"KATAKILLA"

is a Patent and contains the most powerful
Insect Killer ever discovered, which is the
sole property of McDougall's.

Free from Nicotine and other poisons.

In 2/- cartons, each sufficient for 10 galls. Wash.
„ 6/- „ „ „ „ 50 „ „

Sold by

Retailers all over the country, including
all the well-known London Stores,

or direct from

McDOUGALL & ROBERTSON, LTD.,
66/68, PORT ST., MANCHESTER.

KATAKILLA SOLUTION

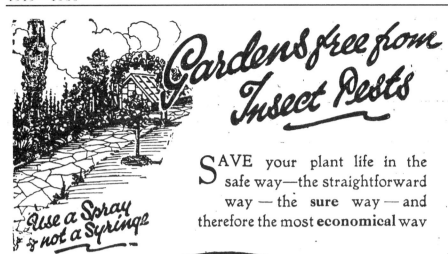

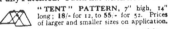

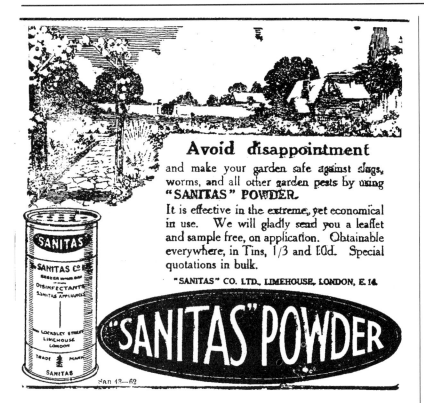

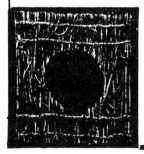

Watering

Water for the garden was still stored in cisterns with a tap or tubs for filling cans by dipping (June 9 1923, page 135). Pumps (7 May 1923, page xix and 1926, page 327) could be used to fill the cisterns as well as for spraying and watering large areas of the garden. Hoses (May 19 1923, page 67), however, allowed watering to become a much easier job, and were available in different grades of varying durablity and price. A fine spray could be achieved with the Penberthy Water Gun (1926, page 196) which was fitted with a spike to allow it to be used as a lawn sprinkler. More complex sprinklers were also available, such as the Success sprinkler from Thomas Gunn (May 19 1923, page 67), with three revolving arms or the Stewart Rain King (1923, page 265) with revolving arms that could also be fixed. Droplet size of the spray was adjustable from coarse to fine, and if low pressure in the water supply was a problem, the Rain King was said to cover a greater area with the same pressure of water than any other sprinkler.

Fertilizers

Fertilizers in pill form made plant feeding more simple: one Fertab pill per month was recommended (May 5 1923, page 20), pushed into the soil near the plant stem. For gardeners who preferred the more established methods of plant feeding, manure was becoming increasingly difficult to obtain. The manufacturers of Adco compost accelerator (1926, page 294) knew where at least part of the blame lay — with the increasing popularity of the motor car — but recommended garden compost (made with Adco accelerator, of course) as 'equal to the best stable manure' (April 30 1924, page 1089).

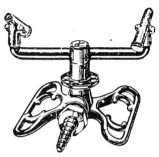
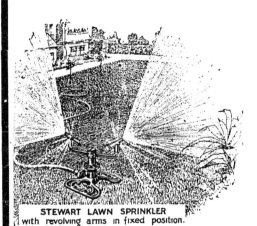
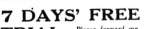

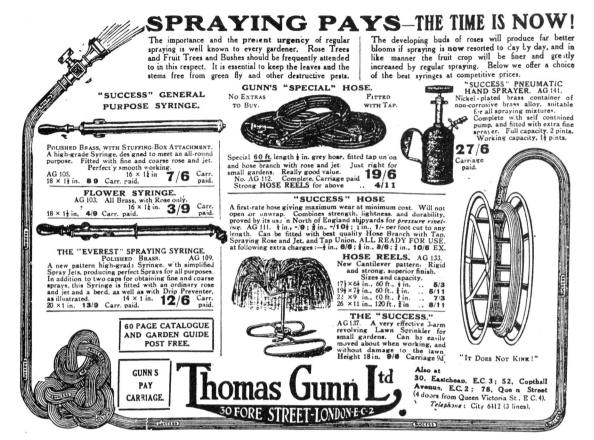

SPRAYING PAYS—THE TIME IS NOW!

The importance and the **present urgency** of regular spraying is well known to every gardener. Rose Trees and Fruit Trees and Bushes should be frequently attended to in this respect. It is essential to keep the leaves and the stems free from green fly and other destructive pests.

The developing buds of roses will produce far better blooms if spraying is **now** resorted to day by day, and in like manner the fruit crop will be finer and greatly increased by regular spraying. Below we offer a choice of the best syringes at competitive prices.

"SUCCESS" GENERAL PURPOSE SYRINGE.

POLISHED BRASS, WITH STUFFING-BOX ATTACHMENT. A high-grade Syringe, designed to meet an all-round purpose. Fitted with fine and coarse rose and jet. Perfectly smooth working.
AG 105. 16 × 1½ in **7/6** Carr. paid.
18 × 1½ in. **8/9** Carr. paid.

FLOWER SYRINGE.
AG 103. All Brass, with Rose only.
16 × 1½ in. **3/9** Carr. paid.
18 × 1½ in. **4/9** Carr. paid.

THE "EVEREST" SPRAYING SYRINGE.
POLISHED BRASS. AG 109.
A new pattern high-grade Syringe, with simplified Spray Jets, producing perfect Sprays for all purposes. In addition to two caps for obtaining fine and coarse sprays, this Syringe is fitted with an ordinary rose and jet and a bend, as well as with Drip Preventer, as illustrated. 14 × 1 in. **12/6** Carr. paid.
20 × 1 in. **13/9** Carr. paid.

60 PAGE CATALOGUE AND GARDEN GUIDE POST FREE.

GUNN'S "SPECIAL" HOSE.
NO EXTRAS TO BUY. FITTED WITH TAP.

Special 60 ft. length ½ in. grey hose, fitted tap union and hose branch with rose and jet. Just right for small gardens. Really good value.
No. AG 112. Complete, Carriage paid **19/6**
Strong **HOSE REELS** for above .. **4/11**

"SUCCESS" PNEUMATIC HAND SPRAYER. AG 141.
Nickel-plated brass container of non-corrosive brass alloy, suitable for all spraying mixtures. Complete with self contained pump, and fitted with extra fine sprayer. Full capacity, 2 pints. Working capacity, 1½ pints.

27/6 Carriage paid.

"SUCCESS" HOSE
A first-rate hose giving maximum wear at minimum cost. Will not open or unwrap. Combines strength, lightness, and durability, proved by its use in North of England shipyards for *pressure riveting*. AG 111. ½ in., **-/9**; ⅝ in., **-/10½**; ¾ in., **1/-** per foot cut to any length. Can be fitted with best quality Hose Branch with Tap, Spraying Rose and Jet, and Tap Union, ALL READY FOR USE, at following extra charges:—½ in., **6/6**; ⅝ in., **8/6**; ¾ in., **10/6** EX.

HOSE REELS. AG 133.
New Cantilever pattern. Rigid and strong, superior finish.
Sizes and capacity.

17½ × 6½ in.,	60 ft.,	½ in.	..	**5/3**
19½ × 7½ in.,	60 ft.,	⅝ in.	..	**5/11**
22 × 9 in.,	60 ft.,	¾ in.	..	**7/3**
26 × 11 in.,	120 ft.,	¾ in	..	**8/11**

THE "SUCCESS."
AG 137. A very effective 3-arm revolving Lawn Sprinkler for small gardens. Can be easily moved about when working, and without damage to the lawn. Height 18 in. **9/6** Carriage 9d.

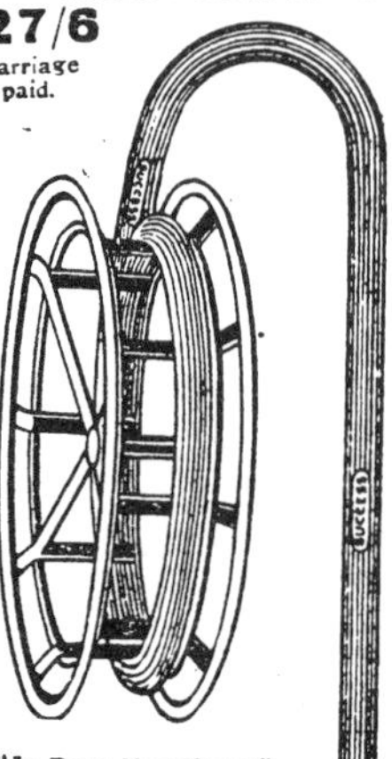

"IT DOES NOT KINK!"

GUNN'S PAY CARRIAGE.

Thomas Gunn Ltd,
30 FORE STREET · LONDON · E·C·2

Also at
30, Eastcheap, E.C. 3; 52, Copthall Avenue, E.C. 2; 78, Queen Street (4 doors from Queen Victoria St., E.C. 4).
Telephone: City 6412 (3 lines).

(MAY 19 1923)

XL PUMP SET

Substantially made in Iron and Brass for hard wear. A splendid outfit for Suction or Spray Work.

£6 10 0
FROM STOCK.

List A free.

C. P. KINNELL & CO., LTD.,
SOUTHWARK ST., LONDON, S.E.1.

(MAY 7 1923)

DOUBLE-ACTING SEMI-ROTARY PUMPS

Pumps fitted any position, adaptable for use in ponds, by riverside, filling cisterns, etc. Fully protected. All working parts enclosed. No cup leathers. Special pattern supplied for removing solid matter and cesspool work.

A.G. 126. Bolted on to 4-leg stands.

Size of Suction and Delivery Pipes screwed.		Maximum capacity per hour galls.		Price.		Without Stand.
No. 1. ¾ in.	..	420	..	**56/6**	..	**27/6**
No. 2. 1 in.	..	540	..	**63/6**	..	**33/6**
No. 3. 1¼ in.	..	660	..	**70/-**	..	**39/6**

Complete catalogue post free.

Carriage paid to goods station England and Wales. Scotland 1/6 extra.

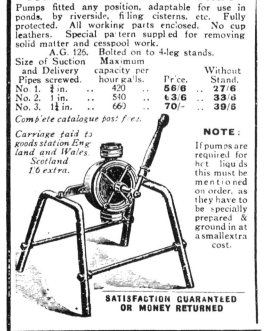

NOTE:
If pumps are required for hot liquids this must be mentioned on order, as they have to be specially prepared & ground in at a small extra cost.

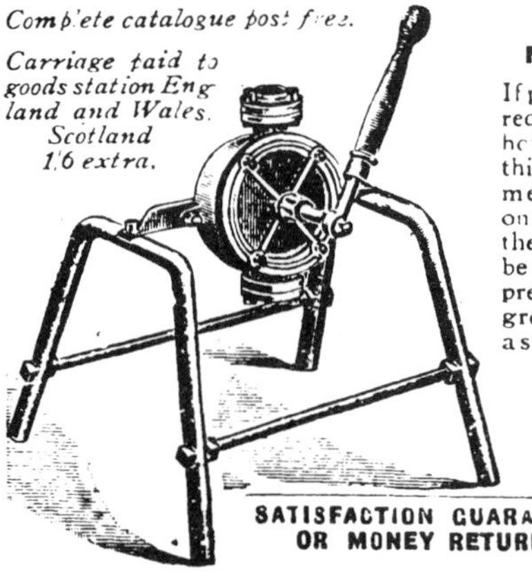

SATISFACTION GUARANTEED OR MONEY RETURNED

(1926)

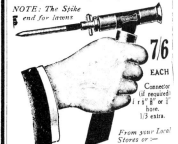

Clothing

Warm, dry feet were important to gardeners in these days before the wellington boot had made its appearance. Strength and durablility were emphasized: 'strong, solid uppers...solid leather double soles with sole and undersole all in one piece...for country wear' (May 7 1921, page 13). Comfortable feet were apparently all-important for all-round good health. Not only corns, bunions and foot troubles, but 'colds, rheumatism, sore throat and kindred ailments' could be prevented, it was implied, by wearing Ruthstein's Waterproof Steel Boots (October 20 1923, page 485).

Boots made from Beva treated leather (1926, page 58) were also claimed to be waterproof, or you could keep your feet dry with slip-on clogs (June 2 1923, page 113) that fitted over your normal shoes. These, too, saved 'damp feet and doctor's bills'. The same company also produced more conventional clogs, lined with 'cosy felt' (May 19 1923, page 67). The name Barbour is still synonymous with waterproof clothing today.

Breeches and gardening aprons were still commonly seen, but smarter trousers 'constructed for hard, grinding wear' (1923, page 177) could also be had. 'Up-to-date' details included raised seams and permanent turn-ups. Although the trousers do not look particularly appropriate for garden work, the back was 'cut in one whole piece, doubling the strength when stooping'; and stooping and kneeling play a large part in gardening, as the Kneeleasy Apron Mat Company (1926, page 451) pointed out. A large inside pocket held a kneeling mat to protect 'hard-working knees'. If you didn't want a full apron in 'gardeners' blue serge', Kneel-on-Air kneeling mats (1926, page 17) were available at less than half the price — and they were 'equally suitable for house work'.

Garden furniture

When the war was over, there was emphasis once more on the garden as a place for enjoyment and relaxation — and for relaxation, garden furniture was essential. Garden benches were popular, whether they were slatted wood on a wrought iron frame (May 19 1923, page 67) or a do-it-yourself job from a parcel of timber (15 June 1921, page xi), 'every joint made and component parts marked'. To make this 'substantial and artistic garden seat' you needed just a screwdriver, a hammer, and one hour of your time. Rail delivery of this self-assembly seat was included in the price, as was common in these days before car ownership was widespread. A free trial period of a week or so may also have been offered, as major items were often bought unseen. If you wanted to inspect goods before buying, large companies such as A. Turrell &

Sons (June 30 1923, page 193) boasted a 'showyard over quarter mile long...2 minutes Forest Hill station'. Here you could obtain rustic style furniture that was a return to the Victorian era — armchairs, tables, benches, shelters, pillars and arches.

Folding chairs appear very similar to today's garden chairs, though the folding mechanism may not be so neat. Slightly soiled canvas chairs (July 28 1923, page 266) 'exactly as supplied for officers' equipment' were available at a bargain price, while striped canvas chairs with arms were a little more expensive. Gunn's (1923, page 21) had a whole range of folding furniture, including the 'C-Esta... the most comfortable chair ever invented' which adjusted to a number of positions, swinging chairs and hammocks with canopies and head rests, and ordinary striped deck chairs with the options of arms and leg rests. For a shady spot or total seclusion there was the Siesta sun awning (with optional curtain) (July 30 1921, page viii) or the Bognor bather tent, in white or striped canvas.

Miscellaneous gardening aids

In 1923, *Amateur Gardening* bemoaned the fact that 'the fine old arts of the domestic still-room have fallen into disuse' (August 11 1923, page 294). They were not recommending that readers distilled their own hooch, but made flower essences — from lavender, peppermint, lilac, roses as well as other herbs and spices. The 'simple, modern apparatus' could be obtained from 'any philosophical instrument maker...being, as it is, an ordinary laboratory apparatus'. The flowers or herbs were heated in the condenser with about four times their weight of water. The tube from the condenser passed through a water jacket through which cold water ran: the condensed steam and essential oil ran into a flask from where the oil could be poured off into bottles for storage.

Once a good crop of fruit had been grown, it had to be stored as long as possible to last through the winter. Special fruit storage trays allowed the fruit to be correctly stored in single layers, with plenty of ventilation to prevent rotting. Taylor's Multi-Tray Cabinet (September 8 1923, page 365) gave easy access to the fruit for use, and allowed regular inspection so that fruits starting to show signs of rotting could be removed quickly. Once the fruit had been used up in spring, the trays could be used for sprouting potatoes before planting. The cabinet had space for 1,000 apples — enough for the produce of a fair-size fruit garden.

If the gardener grew his own vegetables as well, he could have been tempted to buy a Welbank's Boilerette, 'the cooker that looks after itself' (September 15 1923, page 385), in which to cook them. This 'wonder-working invention' (a type of pressure cooker) conserved the 'Valuable Salts, Tonics, Natural Aperients and Life-giving Properties of Vegetables, which are usually washed out and wickedly wasted' preventing and curing 'all kinds of Complaints ranging from Constipation to Cancer'.

No such claims were made for Bird's custard (1923, page 313), though its healthy properties were hinted at. 'Like fresh cream...without any of the risk' and to be preferred to meat and potatoes in hot weather. The manufacturers obviously thought gardeners were a prime source of potential custard eaters: it was one of the most regularly advertised products in *Amateur Gardening* over the years. No doubt it would go with all that home-grown fruit in store.

The correct sowing of seeds saves wasting money on seeds which are sown too thickly, wasting time thinning out crowded seedlings, and the annoyance of 'gappy' rows where sowing has been irregular. There have been many patent seed sowers claiming to have overcome all these problems, none of them with wholesale success. Everyman's Seed Sower (April 8 1922, page 796) sowed any size seed 'from a parsnip to a poppy' and was fitted with 'adjustable regulators' and 'vibratory flanges'. Despite this, a good eye and a steady hand are still the most important attributes for successful sowing.

Plant labelling was another irritation, with labels fading in sunshine and being washed off in rain. Wolff's indelible garden pencils (April 8 1922, page 796) 'withstand all weathers' and 'will not smear or fade' unlike some 'worthless imitations, generally of foreign origin'. The Wolff indelible pencil could also be obtained in the Aintree Garden Label pack along with six dozen labels (April 19 1923, page 1067).

Tidy gardeners who did not want a compost heap could use the Vulcan incinerator (1926, page 55) to keep the garden up to scratch: it would 'burn to ashes a barrow load of refuse with one filling'.

If fruit and vegetables did not make your garden productive enough, then 'every garden should have its beehive' declared Taylors of Welwyn (March 11 1922, page xxv): it was a hobby that was easy, interesting and profitable.

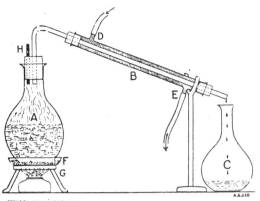

APPARATUS FOR DISTILLING FLOWER ESSENCES.
A. Glass flask. **B.** Condenser. **C.** Receiver. **D.** Cooling jacket. **E.** Tube for carrying off waste water **F.** Frame for flask to rest on. **G.** Lamp. **H.** Plug.

(AUGUST 11 1923)

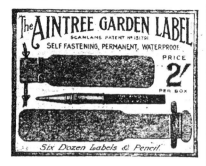

(APRIL 8 1922)

1931–1945

These were difficult years for Britain. The economy was slowly starting to recover after the depression, but another preoccupation soon arose — the dangerous rise of fascism in Europe, culminating in another world war just twenty-one years after the end of the first. This war was to be entirely different from the Great War, directly involving the British civilian public for the first time.

The difference is obvious from the pages of *Amateur Gardening*. World War I was mentioned only occasionally at the time — notable horticulturists who had been killed at the Front, or the effects of German gas on vegetation — but from the very outset of World War II, war permeated every issue. The Dig for Victory campaign (1940, page 413) had been started in the First World War, but had met with some resistance. Then *Amateur Gardening*, and some of its advertisers who stood to lose by the campaign, had expressed the opinion that the government had been over-hasty in urging the population to dig up their ornamental lawns and borders to replace them with vegetables. There were no such reservations the second time round and while ornamental horticulture still had its place in the magazine, food production was by far and away the most important aspect of war-time gardening.

Garden tools

Soil cultivation was still one of the most back-breaking aspects of gardening, particularly for vegetable growers, and there continued to be a range of products designed to take the hard labour out of the job. The adjustable potato ridger (5th May 1934, page 27) claimed to be easier, quicker and better than digging. For cultivating between crops, Cope's expanding cultivator (14th May 1938, page 1) was 'better and easier than hoeing'. The tines could be adjusted to varying widths while in use, enabling the cultivator to be used between crops at different row spacings. The Planet Junior Jiffy Hoe (31st May 1941, page 8) was easier still and as increasing numbers of novice gardeners began growing vegetables in 1941, there must have been a ready market for any implement that promised to make the work less strenuous. The advertisement warns that early ordering is advisable as only a limited number of hoes is available — a message that was to be repeated more and more often as the war progressed. Smallholders who had access to a horse or pony could make use of the Landmark pony plough (9th Dec 1941, page 16), 'a real plough...yet light and manageable'. Ease of use was important as implements were increasingly used by women who were left to take charge at home while the men were away fighting.

For those who still relied on hand tools, the Easi-Digger (7th November 1944, page 4) promised to 'cut out all those back-bendings and back-aches'. Fitted to a normal spade or fork, the Easi-Digger used leverage to make the job lighter, though the manufacturers admitted that the new technique took practice to perfect. One-handed digging was possible and to prove it, preference was given to orders from one-armed ex-Servicemen. The single-handled, multi-headed tool set was still about: Young's set (15th August 1944, page 16) had 'one handle, five tools, ten uses'. Strength and durability are always good selling points, and the Neer-A-Weld weldless garden fork (1930, page 885) proved its point with an acrobatic display by some members of the workforce.

A lot of damage can be done to plants by careless transplanting: the rootball must remain intact as far as possible to avoid a setback. A transplanter (7th June 1941, page 3) that lifts plants complete with all roots and soil would certainly give them a better chance, though whether this implement would save time as well is another matter. A similar tool was also available for seedlings (19th May 1934, page x).

Seed sowers made their appearance once again. An earlier model (28th February 1930, page xxv) was fitted with a plunger and spring to distribute the seeds evenly, while the Gem (9th May 1944, page 2) is of a simpler design. Simple tools are often the best and few could be simpler than the chromium-plated Wydger (22nd October 1938, page xxi). Invaluable for 'widging', it was suitable for all small plants but particularly for alpines, and was made by Rolcut — better known for their pruners.

Lots of gardeners fail to handle a hoe correctly, using it to dig weeds up rather than gliding it over the surface to decapitate them with a well-sharpened blade. The Topper hoe (9th May 1944, page 6) was a rather revolutionary design that helped to ensure it was used in the right way. The blade ran flat along the soil, guided by a front skid; it could be turned to be used as a push hoe or pull hoe, or set at an angle for working between narrow rows.

Weeding was another back-breaking job, and lawn weeds were a particular problem in the days before selective weedkillers. A long-handled, lever action weeder (11th June 1938, page 150) promised to make the job easy enough to be undertaken with one hand in your pocket.

Though secateurs replaced knives for many pruning jobs, there were still plenty of uses for a good gardening knife. The I-XL range (15th November 1930, page xxiii) included budding and grafting knives, and boasted blades sharpened on one side only for better control and a cleaner cut. Ridged handles gave a better grip, but professionals and keen gardeners who used their knives for extended periods preferred smooth wood handles that were less likely to cause blisters. Wilkinson Sword pruning shears (1930, page 975), with their large, parrot-bill type blades, were 'keen as a cut-throat' and their handles were long in order to give extra leverage to increase the cutting power. Milton's grass cutter and hedge trimmer (19th May 1934, page 84) was literally razor-sharp, being fitted with six razor blades. It was supplied with a very necessary guard to slip over the blades when not in use, and you could use your old razor blades to renew the cutting edges as necessary.

Before pre-packed bags of sterile sowing and potting composts were freely available from garden centres, garden soil had to be used for most purposes. Weeds, soil pests and diseases were common problems, but they could be overcome by soil sterilization at home using the Cope Portable Steam Soil Steriliser (7th May 1938, page 1). Sterile soil was mainly necessary for potting certain delicate plants and for raising seedlings.

The fitting of pneumatic tyred wheels to wheelbarrows was a real advance in making gardening easier, instantly converting the hard slog of wheeling heavy loads over soft or uneven ground into a simple task. In 1930 you could replace the old wooden or iron wheel with a new Dunlop wheel (7th March 1930, page xviii) supplied complete with axle. Four years later, the 'new pattern' garden barrow (26th May 1934, page xii) was far less practical. Meant specifically for women, it would be much more at home shopping in the high street, and must have had very limited use in the garden. Rubber-tyred wheels were available, and recommended by the makers in preference to the cheaper wooden wheels. By 1941 a more sensible design was being promoted as 'ideal for ladies' (28th June 1941, page 6). Though still fitted with an iron wheel as standard, it had rubber wheels as an optional extra. The Sims steel barrow (30th March 1935, page xliii) offered plain rubber, rib-stud and 'buoyant' tyres, and the handles and legs of the barrow folded away for storage in small gardens and confined spaces.

In 1935, Qualcast claimed there were already over one million users of their machines. All their mowers were now fitted with ball-bearings (30th March 1935, page xi), from the cheaper side-wheel models to the more expensive roller model Panther, complete with grassbox. Roller models had the advantage of cutting right over lawn edges, which side-wheel mowers could not do. Qualcast promised spare parts in 24 hours, and gave a three year guarantee. DB mowers (30th March 1935, page xliii) — also fitted with ball-bearings — went much further: their machines were 'guaranteed for ever'. The cutting cylinders could be easily removed for resharpening.

As more and more lawns were turned over to vegetables in the war years, mowers became less important. In 1940, Royal Enfield (18th May 1940, page xviii) were steadfastly claiming 'English lawns will outlive wartime' and urging gardeners to 'prepare peacetime lawns with a Royal Enfield'. Unfortunately it was to be a long time before gardeners were thinking about preparing their gardens for peacetime, and the manufacture of lawn mowers was very soon to be a casualty of the war effort in any case. Manufacturers continued to take out advertisements in *Amateur Gardening* to keep their names in gardeners' minds even though their products were no longer available, but by May 1944 adverts started to talk more hopefully and confidently of peacetime, advising readers to 'keep in touch with your dealer after the war to find out when manufacture restarts' (9th May 1944, page 2).

Lawns do not just need mowing of course. Rolling was commonly practised to keep lawns and paths level, and the 'dashed ingenious' Ironcrete roller (1930, page 846) incorporated a detachable mud scraper to make it self cleaning. Sweeping improved lawn-mowing by raising the grasses to meet the mower blades and scattering worm casts. The cylindrical shape of the Easiway sweeper (1930, page 846) allowed it to be rotated to provide a new surface as the old one wore down.Or if you wanted to do your sweeping and rolling in one operation, the Little Giant roller (1930, page 885) was for you. Since the roller followed the brush, the only practical purpose of sweeping was to distribute worm casts before they were spread by the roller, which usually resulted in patches of turf dying.

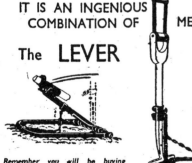

Step on it !

Dig Now — Don't Delay — Get your garden ready to grow your own vegetables — especially the kinds you can store. Apply to your local Council for an allotment and dig with all your might. Vegetables will be scarcer. Victory may well be won by the country with the most food. It is up to every man and woman to step on it now and make every garden a VICTORY GARDEN.

DIG for victory NOW!

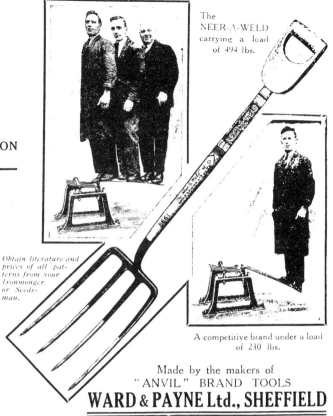

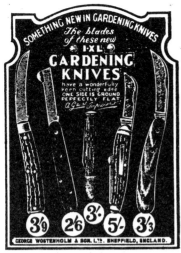
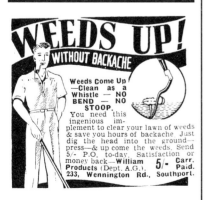

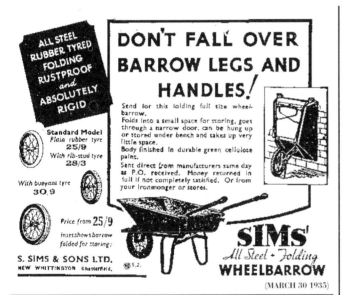

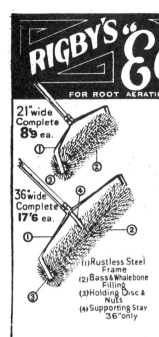

Fertilizers

Ensuring heavy crops was especially important during the war, and fertilizers played their part in getting the maximum from every plant. But even before the war, gardeners were being promised extraordinary results from a new discovery — radioactive plant food (5th May 1934, page 45). 'The most startling news for gardeners ever published' was hardly an exaggeration. This 'plant energiser' was said to be a 'clean dry powder possessing radioactive properties...clean to handle and has no smell whatever'. Like the 'horticultural electricty' of the Sun Ray Magnets in 1915, radioactive fertilizer promised plants that would 'grow with the dark, luscious green of vigorous life, and finally burst into a profusion of large, glorious blooms, intensely brilliant in colour and perfect in fragrance'. Radioliser did not rely completely on its radioactive properties for results: it did contain normal plant foods as well.

By the time the war was under way, such gimmicks had disappeared. Reminding readers of the importance of the National 'Grow More Food' effort, the distributors of 99-9 soluble blood fertilizer (11th May 1940, page 46) were at pains to point out that it was not a chemical, though it was a 'scientific product'. Suspending a sack of manure in a water barrel was the old way of producing a liquid fertilizer, with inconsistent and presumably smelly results. Liquinure (28th June 1941, page 3) was the better way to liquid manure —'new, clean, odourless'.

By 1941, Eclipse fertiliser (7th June 1941, page 8) was in trouble: the raw materials for its manufacture and packaging could no longer be imported. 'The time has arrived when we must call a halt' said the company, advising gardeners to buy existing stocks while they could. The Merchant Navy was fully occupied trying to bring home other vital supplies, as the manufacturers of Clay's fertilizer (10th May 1941, page 23) pointed out: all gardeners could help by growing more food — aided by Clay's fertilizer, of course.

As well as food, plants need water, and during times of drought it is essential to get the water to where it is needed, at the roots of the plant. The Aquatern (2nd July 1938, page xiv) did just that, and allowed watering to take place in full sun with no fear of the water evaporating.

New Radio-Active Plant-Growing Discovery

Makes the Pictures on the Seed Packets Come True!

Greatest advance in gardening for 25 years.

HERE is the most startling news for keen gardeners ever published in any paper, anywhere, any time.

It is the news of the discovery of a wonderful *Radio-Active* Plant-Growing Preparation which "charges" the roots of plants with radio-active energy, making them grow more vigorously, develop more perfectly, and bloom more freely than has ever been possible before except for the most expert professional gardeners.

This new discovery is called RADIOLISER, and actual plant-growing tests over a period of three years have proved that it **literally makes the pictures on the seed packets come true.**

With the aid of Radioliser every amateur can make his or her garden rich and luxurious with glorious Roses, Sweet Peas, and all varieties of Flowers. Even though you have only a small plot, you can make it more beautiful this year than it has ever been before—a source of pride and joy to you, and the admiration and envy of your neighbours.

All you have to do.

RADIOLISER Plant Energiser is a clean dry powder possessing *radio-active* properties.

It is absolutely clean to handle and has no smell whatever—a point which lady gardeners especially will appreciate.

You simply sprinkle Radioliser round the plant, lightly hoe it into the soil, then water the soil as usual.

Then the Radio-Active properties of Radioliser get to work.

It sinks down among the roots and "charges" them with *radio-active* energy in the form of three different kinds of rays (known to scientists as Alpha, Beta and Gamma rays). And just as the radio-active emanations from the waters of famous Health Spas invigorate and energise the human system so these rays emitted by the radio-active substance in Radioliser flood the plants with life-giving energy. In a short while the stems and leaves of the plants thicken and grow with the dark, luscious green of vigorous life, and finally burst into a profusion of large, glorious blooms, intensely brilliant in colour and perfect in fragrance.

Compared with "Radiolised" plants, other plants growing in the same soil look more like weeds, so marked is the difference. (See illustration on right.)

Radioliser is a "balanced" Plant Food.

Radioliser Plant Energiser—in addition to being *radio-active*—is a complete and perfectly balanced plant food containing all the essential elements of perfect plant growth. Moreover, these essential ingredients have been blended in such a way in Radioliser that no one feature of the plant is "forced" at the expense of another, as is usually the case with the now old-fashioned "fertiliser." Preparations which contain an excessive quantity of Nitrogen, for instance, cause an immediate and rapid growth of the stems and leaves at the expense of the blooms, thus resulting in a tall, "straggly" plant, which produces only small, scattered flowers. In Radioliser Plant Energiser, however, the quantity of Nitrogen is carefully balanced **in relation to the other ingredients,** so that the plant grows evenly and sturdily, and develops in a perfectly natural way. In the same way each of

the other ingredients is so controlled that it contributes its proper share to the general welfare of the plant, and so develops its full perfection in every way.

A further important feature of Radioliser Plant Energiser is the fact that it is composed partly of soluble and partly of insoluble "foods." The importance of this will be realised when it is understood that many ordinary fertilisers which are

(Above)
WITHOUT
Radioliser
Note the weak, "leggy" growth and small ragged blooms of plant above — grown WITHOUT Radioliser.

WITH
Radioliser
Note the amazing difference in the size and profusion of the blooms, the richness of the foliage and strong, vigorous stems of the "Radiolised" plant on right.

Every carton of Radioliser contains a 12-page booklet telling you exactly how to "Radiolise" over 65 different flowering plants. You cannot go wrong! So why not make sure of getting the utmost value out of the money you have invested on seeds and plants by growing them all to glorious perfection this new and easy way?

soluble or are supplied to the plant in the form of a solution, actually do more harm than good. The reason is that they overfeed the plant for a short time, which is followed by a period of starvation, during which the plant gets no food at all, because these solutions are quickly exhausted and washed down past the roots of the plant by heavy rains. This alternate feeding and starving is generally recognised as the worst form of feeding, whether for plants or animals.

In the case of Radioliser Plant Energiser, however, the proportion of soluble and insoluble "foods" is so balanced that while some of its nutriment is made immediately available to the plant by means of the soluble ingredients, the remainder is only made available gradually as it is slowly broken down by chemical action in the soil. Thus, Radioliser Plant Energiser provides the plant with a steady supply of nourishment during the whole of its growth instead of at spasmodic intervals.

Make this simple test forthwith.

Why not be the first in your district to try RADIOLISER, and prove for yourself how it doubles the beauty and luxuriance of your plants and flowers?

Try a 1/6 carton of Radioliser Plant Energiser and "Radiolise" just a few plants in your garden, leaving others untreated. Then see how the "Radiolised" plants outstrip the others in every way. See how Radioliser brings a richer colour to the greenery and how, under its radio-active influence your flower-beds burst forth into masses of gorgeous blooms, colour-perfume - and - petal-perfect.

See how your climbers such as Sweet Peas, etc., array themselves with thousands of rainbow-hued blossoms on long, strong stalks convenient for cutting.

See how your borders and rockeries become solid masses of glowing colour.

Everyone who possesses a garden, however small (even though it be only a window box), can make this Radioliser trial, and in every case be delighted with the way this odourless and clean-to-handle powder improves every plant, flower, or fern.

Radioliser Plant Energiser is obtainable from Seedsmen, Nurserymen, Ironmongers, Corn Dealers and Chemists in 1/6 and 3/- cartons. Or, in case of difficulty, you can obtain either size direct from **Radioliser, 300 Adelphi, Salford, Manchester.**

Radioliser for LAWNS Too!

A special form of Radioliser called Radioliser LAWN TONIC—is available for lawns. Like Radioliser Plant Energiser it possesses Radio-Active properties and contains special "foods" which nourish the finer grasses only and produce close, even growth of carpet-like smoothness free from coarse grasses and weeds. Obtainable in 1/6 and 3/- cartons, every carton contains full instructions and many useful hints on lawn cultivation.

(MAY 5 1934)

THEY ALL HELP—USUALLY!

THE above diagram indicates seven different countries in four different Continents whose resources are represented in every bag of "Eclipse" you buy from your local seedsman in peace-time. Automatically, then, it also gives an indication of some of the problems which we as the manufacturers are having to contend with in maintaining the supply.

It can be taken for granted, for example, that we should not import potash from Germany if we could get it locally, nor should we send to India for the jute for the bags if it was grown in this country. It follows, then, that even when normal supplies are completely cut off, we still have to search overseas for alternative producers, with all the problems and difficulties which ocean transport entails under present conditions.

No-one can be surprised, then, to hear that supplies are not quite as plentiful as in peace-time; in fact, the marvel is that we have been able to get as near as we have to pre-war production. It speaks volumes for the Royal Navy and their efficiency in getting convoys home.

Nevertheless, the time has arrived when we must call a halt. Supplies of certain raw materials are exhausted, and we are down to bare boards, and you remember there is an old adage which says—"Bricks cannot be made without straw." Even so, however, we are pleased to be able to add that this bit of bad news need not worry our amateur gardener friends just yet.

In the first place, those who know the value of the

"*Eclipse*" COMPOUND FISH MANURE

for all garden and vegetable crops will already have made sure of their seasonal requirements, whilst those who have not yet done so will be able to get what they want from their seedsmen if they "go to it."

Actually our seedsmen friends have done wonders in helping us to get stocks moved from this vulnerable corner of the country, but even their supplies are being rapidly depleted and are not likely to be replenished before the Autumn. A few shillings spent now, therefore, in laying in a little reserve is likely to prove money well spent, and, in any case, it will avoid disappointment later on.

Should you experience any difficulty in your particular town, let us know, and we will advise you at once if we know of a conveniently-situated supply.

Sole Registered Manufacturers :—

THE HUMBER FISHING & FISH MANURE CO., LTD., Stoneferry Offices, HULL

(*Contractors to H.M. Government.*)

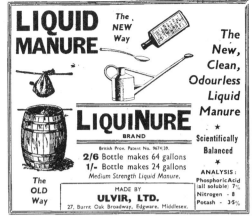

LIQUID MANURE
The NEW Way

LiquiNure
BRAND
British Prov. Patent No. 9674/39.

2/6 Bottle makes 64 gallons
1/- Bottle makes 24 gallons
Medium Strength Liquid Manure.

MADE BY
ULVIR, LTD.
27, Burnt Oak Broadway, Edgware, Middlesex.

The OLD Way

The New, Clean, Odourless Liquid Manure
★
Scientifically Balanced
★
ANALYSIS:
Phosphoric Acid (all soluble) 7%
Nitrogen - 8
Potash - 3·5%

Get to the ROOT of your watering troubles

WATER your plants in the SUN and never fear drought
with the

Aquatern
ROOT WATERER

AMAZING RESULTS are achieved with the "AQUATERN." It saves time, trouble, and makes watering a pleasure. The overall height of 3 feet enables you to get water to the roots of a small plant to a large tree, in **30 seconds**. The only effective way of watering **Rockeries.**

Strongly made in Solid Polished Brass, with attachment for ½in. Hose.
12 MONTHS' GUARANTEE.

Price 15/6 POST FREE

With Universal Fitting for ½in., ⅝in. and ¾in. Hose, 1/3 extra.

SMALL JETS FOR SEEDLINGS 2/-.

Write for Descriptive Leaflet.

THE IRRIGATING & FERTILIZING TOOL CO.,
16, Shepperton Road, London, N.1.
Telephone: Clissold 1474.
Special Terms to Horticulture Societies.

Pests and diseases

One way of dealing with lawn weeds was to apply weed killer selectively, to each weed in turn. The Ricco weeder (21st February 1930, page xxxi), used with Ricco herbicide, allowed you to treat lawn weeds without stooping, at a rate of 3,000 weeds per hour. The Duxbury Weeder (1940, page ix) on the other hand, removed the weeds physically, collecting them automatically, but only at the rate of some 600 per hour. The Luto (18th July 1944, page 16) both applied weed killer to the roots and removed the top growth of weeds from the grass — though you would have had to pick the severed weed tops up yourself.

Many sprayers still required the use of a bucket for the solution to be sprayed. The Nesthill Universal Sprayer (1930, page 1083) made a virtue of its versatility, pointing out that you could not only use it for spraying fruit trees, but for whitewashing buildings, creosoting fences and washing windows and cars as well. Mysto were still supplying similar bucket sprayers in 1944, (30th May 1944, page 12) though they also produced a more portable 'non-splash' model, as well as a syringe for smaller jobs. A 'definite improvement on the old type handspray', Enots Floraspray (5th May 1934 xxii) looked like an oil can, but produced a 'very fine mist' at 'exceedingly high pressure'. The Wasp sprayer (23rd June 1934, page xxi) advertised itself as 'something new...a spray container that is really portable'. Unlike similar models, this sprayer did not require continuous pumping during operation. It was used on fruit trees and garden plants — not as a domestic fly and wasp killer as the advertisement might seem to suggest.

Insecticides and fungicides were still available in powder form, too, and a range of powder blowers was available (5th May 1934, page xi). The Baker Metal Stopper bellows (21st May 1938, page xvii) is remarkably similar to powder bellows of the previous century. The Acme Powder Blower (17th May 1941, page 6) could be operated by one hand requiring merely 'a flick of the wrist'. But in 1941, sprayer manufacturers, too, were applying themselves 'wholeheartedly to the National production effort' and sprayers, like so many other items, were in short supply. Enots (1941 21st June 1941, page 20) looked forward to a return to 'quieter moments' with a wistful picture of a peaceful English scene.

Some garden pests could be scared, rather than sprayed, away. Children's windmills are often used as birdscarers, but here was a purpose-made 'flying propeller' — the Flitafast (1930, page 1090). Apart from the 'gaily coloured wings', it was fitted with a rattle to add to its scaring power, and was even said to work on rats and mice. As a further bonus, it was 'not an eyesore but an ornament'. The menacing-looking Glitterer bird scarer (1935, page 842) not only had eyes that shone and glittered in the light, but was fitted with a spring that enabled it 'to leap about in the most terrifying manner'. A jangling bell added to the effect 'to the terror of the birds' and unwary passers-by, no doubt. If cats themselves were your problem, Shoo pepper dust (May 7th 1938, page 25) was 'harmless but most effective', and was also said to work on dogs, mice, rabbits, slugs and birds.

But 'poisonous potions' were still the choice of most gardeners for dealing with pests and diseases. There was still no requirement to state the active ingredients of pesticides, and advertisers frequently used recommendations to convince gardeners of their products' properties. Clensel insecticide (5th May 1934, page 20) was endorsed by well-known plantsmen Suttons and Dobbies while Abol (23 June 1934, page 197) was 'used in the Royal Gardens'. In 1940, garden pests took on the identity of that other great national enemy: slugs, snails, aphids and caterpillars appeared adorned with swastikas (18th May 1994, page 48), while Derrothan and Derromulsion pesticides flew the Union Jack. Boltac greasebands (31st October 1944, page 15) also took on a military guise — 'no enemy bridgeheads over these!'. And no prizes for guessing the identity of the rat (28th December 1940, page iii). The cost of damage caused by rats across the country was estimated at £30 million, a sum that could be ill-afforded by a country at war. No wonder Local Authorities were eager to help push across the message that the only good rat was a dead rat.

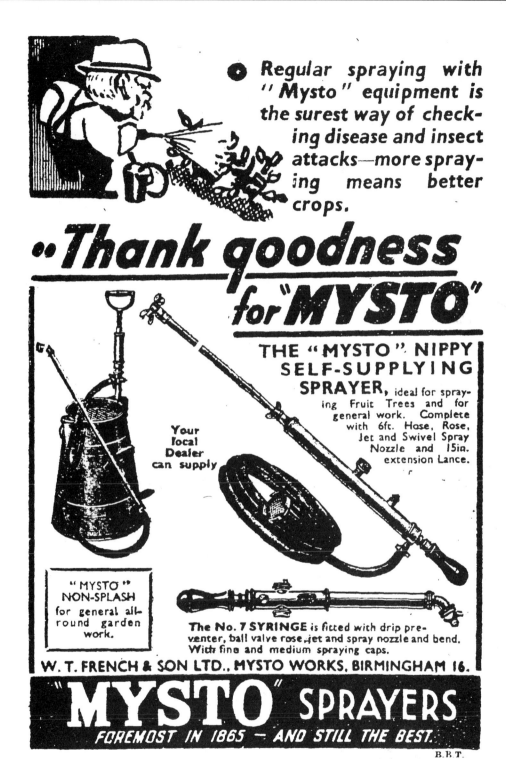

DESTROY THOSE GARDEN PESTS THIS SIMPLE EFFECTIVE WAY

PRICE 1/- EACH
POST FREE

This inexpensive bellows is invaluable for the dispensing of fine dusting powders. It is small, light, handy to use, and has nothing mechanical to get out of order.

The box-like container, which is easily opened by removing the lid, can be filled with any powder you care to buy.

Bellows, without powder, can be obtained from Horticultural sundriesmen, or direct from the makers. Wholesale enquiries invited

The **BAKER METAL STOPPER** Co LTD

Hadley Street • Key Hill • BIRMINGHAM

(MAY 21 1938)

CATS ... CATS ... CATS . . . .

DOGS, MICE, RABBITS, SLUGS, BIRDS, etc.

save your garden from their attention

TAKE THE RECENT BROADCAST ADVICE OF MR. C. H. MIDDLETON

use

PEPPER DUST

You can obtain supplies of

"SHOO" BRAND PEPPER DUST

(Harmless, but most effective)

from

ARTHUR J. HARRIS & CO., LTD.

Crosby Spice Mills, Gt. Crosby, Liverpool, 23

3 lbs. ... 2/-   14 lbs. ... 5/-

FULL DIRECTIONS ENCLOSED

Carriage Paid. Cash with order

Salts

(MAY 7 1938)

Beware of Imitations and REAP WHAT YOU SOW

By buying the one and only Efficient Bird Scarer (Glitterer), whose eyes shine and glitter in the light. Fitted with a spring which enables it to leap about in the most terrifying manner. At the same time

Retails **6d.**

the bell rings and adds to the fearsome and 100% Effective Article, and to the Terror of the Birds. Retails at the same price, 6d.

Large ones also obtainable at 2/- and 2/3, with improvements.

Obtainable from all Seedsmen, Nurserymen and Florists.

Generous trade terms. Full particulars from Sole Agents. Messrs.

CORRY & CO., LTD., GAINSFORD STREET SHAD THAMES, S.E.1

(FEBRUARY 9 1935)

The DUXBURY LAWN WEEDER

A Marvellous Invention

Patent No. 479616

5/- EACH POST 6d

NO INCREASE IN PRICE

- Collects weeds automatically.
- Up to 600 weeds per hour.
- No bending, no stooping.
- Hundreds of testimonials.
- The finest lawn weeder ever marketed.
- Makes weeding a pleasure.

FROM ALL IRONMONGERS. If any difficulty apply to Sole Manufacturers, Thomas Staniforth & Co., Ltd., Severquick Works, Hackenthorpe, Sheffield.

(1940)

SCARE THE BIRDS and SAVE YOUR SEEDS

BY USING

"FLITAFAST" (REGD.) FLYING PROPELLERS

GAILY COLOURED WINGS THAT REVOLVE WITH THE SLIGHTEST WIND.

○ ○ ○

BIRDS WILL NOT COME NEAR THESE SCARES.

FITTED WITH A RATTLE THAT FRIGHTENS THE BIRDS AS THE GAILY COLOURED WINGS REVOLVE.

○ ○ ○

RATS AND MICE ARE ALSO SCARED AWAY

18 IN. STICK. Patent No. 26969. Reg. Design 748648

NOT AN EYESORE BUT AN ORNAMENT

A dozen in a large garden will keep Seeds, Fruit Trees and Soft Fruits quite safe from all interference. Nothing to go wrong. Will stand all weathers and last for years.

M. M. writes :—" Since using a few of your 'Flitafast' I never see a bird near my seeds."

F. W. B. says :—" My Fruit Trees have been left severely alone since using your scares."

A. E. P. writes :—" Before using 'Flitafast' Scares my garden was troubled with mice. They have all been scared away since."

1 Doz. Assorted, Gaily Coloured 2/9, Post 6d.

2 „   „   „   „   5/-   „ 6d.

3 „   „   „   „   7/- Post Free

DESPATCHED PER RETURN IN STRONG BOX.

Trade Enquiries Invited.

SOLE MAKERS :

CASCELLOID LTD., Britannia Works, Cobden St., LEICESTER

(APRIL 1930)

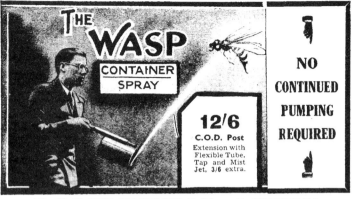

Greenhouses

Timber greenhouses, such as those sold by Prattens of Midsomer Norton (22nd October 1938, page xxii), were still the most common, but sectional steel greenhouses were becoming increasingly popular (16th July 1938, page viii and 17th September 1938, page xx). Steel greenhouses admitted more light because of the thinner framework: though more durable than wood the steel frame still needed painting to protect it, unlike the aluminium greenhouses which followed. Steel greenhouses were more expensive than timber: a Pelham 8ft x 5ft timber greenhouse (22nd October 1938, page xxii) cost £8 14s 0d, while an 8ft x 6ft steel house (17th September 1938, page xx) cost £9 12s 6d — but the steel greenhouse was delivered free to your nearest railway station.

In May 1940, shortages were beginning to make themselves felt. Waltons greenhouses (11th May 1940, page viii) were still available — and at pre-war prices — but stocks were 'very limited'. By the following year, manufacturers such as Boulton & Paul (12th August 1941, page 4) were 'exclusively engaged on War Work, Doing our bit for Victory' and their products were no longer available to the home gardener. 'Earlier wars have never shattered our tradition. Neither will this one' they proclaimed confidently, and correctly, as it turned out. War brought other problems, too: you could protect your plants from glass shattered by bombing raids with Anti-Blast transparent paint (1940, page 265), which did not interfere with light transmission through the glass.

Greenhouses could be heated very simply with portable paraffin heaters such as the Midnight Sun (November 8th 1940, page xxii), which would burn for 24 hours without attention, but more modern methods were making an appearance. The Daisy gas heater (1st October 1938, page xix) promised 'flowers all the winter...no stoking...practically indestructible', while the Electro-cult electric heater (4th November 1941, page 2) claimed to be 'the cheapest method of greenhouse heating', though at over £9 for the smallest size it cost nearly as much as a small greenhouse itself.

Gardeners without a greenhouse could extend the growing season with cloches, which Chase (16th May 1944, page 20) claimed to be 'doubling and trebling output': all-important during the war. For 6d, growers could learn how cloches were helping to win the war from a booklet entitled 'Cloches v. Hitler'. Sunralite plastic cloches were also available (3rd November 1934, page 565) and their unbreakable and lightweight properties were being promoted in 1934. Windolite glass substitute (1st December 1934, page xix) claimed to be better in almost every way than glass, and cheaper into the bargain. Over half a century later, however, with plastics being used in ways pre-war gardeners could never have dreamed of, glass is still the number one material for glazing greenhouses.

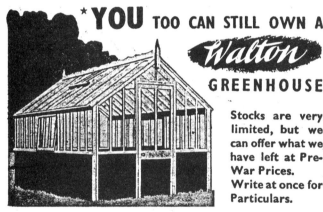

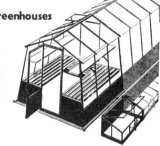

Gardeners' clothing

Leather boots were still used for gardening in 1930: John White's boots (1930, page 539) boasted the brand name 'Impregnable' and were said to be specially made for use in the garden. 'Honest materials and skilled British craftsmenship' ensured they would stand up to hard wear 'without losing their looks or their comfort'.

By 1940, rubber boots (23rd November 1940, page v) were more commonplace — but like so many other items at that time, they were becoming difficult to obtain 'for those who are not in uniform'. The clog (14th June 1941, page 22) still had its devotees, and was specially recommended for cold, damp, comfortless air raid shelters as well as garden work. Soles were of beechwood, but they could be fitted with rubber for half a crown (2s 6d) extra. Or for 'the toughest boots you ever purchased' there were 'slightly used Army Boots (16th September 1941, page 2), completely renovated by government contractors'. They were presumably not tough enough for the army to want them, but at least they required no precious clothing coupons. A few navy and airforce rejects were also available.

'To be comfortably clad helps the job', and the right apparel in which to dig for victory included a pair of made-to-measure breeches (17th May 1941, page 6). The rapidly escalating prices of wartime Britain are reflected in the exhortation to 'send now before prices rise again'. Similar breeches had been available for almost half the price in 1934.

Miscellaneous odds and ends

In 1930, smart men wore a buttonhole — 'both the King and the Prince of Wales' among them — and to keep a buttonhole fresh, Rowe's Reservoir Flower Holder (1930, page 703) was ideal. Available in silver, gilded silver or solid gold, the flower holder was 'quite different to the ordinary flimsy article' and made a 'charming little present for a man'. A velvet-lined case was available as an optional extra.

The attractive but fragile rope-edged Victorian edging tiles were being replaced by 'garden edging of the future' — galvanized steel sections (10th November 1934, page xxiv) which fitted together and were easily shaped to fit curved paths and beds. Wood had also been used for edging, but apart from being very prone to rotting, it also provided a good home for a variety of insect pests, which steel did not.

The pre-sown lawn (7th May 1938, page 19) was hailed as an 'amazing revolution in lawn culture' which was 'sweeping the country'. It was another of those revolutions that failed to stick, though similar products have reappeared sporadically since. Since the major work in making a new lawn lies in the soil preparation, the pre-sown lawn mats did not offer any distinct advantage: the same soil preparation was necessary for both methods. The seed was at least safe from birds, however. It would, in any case, not be very long before lawns were disappearing, converted to vegetable plots in the campaign to grow more food.

Vegetables could be started off indoors and planted out as soon the weather allowed in soil blocks made by the Seedaset tool (7th April 1941, page 7). No pots were necessary, and seedlings could be transplanted without root disturbance, ensuring they got away to a good start. Vegetable growers were already struggling in 1941, since for the second year running, there had been difficulties in obtaining sufficient seed potatoes to meet the greatly increased demand. Transport difficulties and hard frosts compounded the problem, and potato growers were asked to forego the pleasures of an early harvest, and instead to leave the tubers in the ground until they reached a good size. Quantity had become far more important than quality.

Eggs were also scarce throughout the war, and many gardeners who had the space kept their own chickens, feeding them mainly on kitchen waste and food scraps. Under the tantalizing promise of 'eggs for all' baby chicks were advertised by the dozen (31st May 1941, page 20). Light Sussex and White Leghorns were the most expensive, with Rhode Island Reds and crosses a little cheaper. The chicks came with a 'free leaflet explaining how to rear'.

Timber was another product in short supply during the war, and its price rose accordingly. Nodek concrete fence repair posts (21st May 1941, page 5) held fences upright 'against the strongest March wind that ever blew' and helped avoid costly and difficult repairs.

Sticking plasters were one idea that really did take off. In 1938 waterproof Band-Aids (3rd September 1938, page 372) were being advertised as particularly suitable for gardeners. 'You can go on working — planting out, pulling weeds, watering — no dirt, germs or moisture can get past the Band-Aid plaster'. Sticking plasters were quicker to apply and more hygienic than bandages.

During wartime, it was not only your duty to grow as much fruit and vegetables as you possibly could, while suffering shortages of all sorts of essential items cheerfully, it was also your patriotic duty to stay healthy. The Iodine Educational Bureau was keen to promote the antiseptic properties of iodine (16th September 1941, page 2), recommending it for a wide range of ailments from sore throats to sore feet. Women were largely responsible for gardening during the war years, as an advert for hand cream noted (11th May 1940, page 29): 'We're doing more work in the garden now — harder work than some of us have ever done before'. A tube of Glymiel kept 'handy with the gardening tools' promised a little comfort for work-roughened hands.

When a housewife was not busy in the garden, she had to turn her attention to the kitchen, and dealing with the harvest. 'Bottle all you can and help the National effort!...The Nation demands that you waste no food, so GO TO IT!' Snap Vacuum Closures (1940, page 245) enabled you to vacuum-pack fruit for a longer shelf life — and unlike jam, no precious sugar was needed.

Growing your own vegetables gave you a reasonable supply of fresh, healthy food, but meat was harder to come by. For a generation raised on the idea of 'meat and two veg' as the only proper meal, a diet heavy on vegetables and exceedingly light on meat must have seemed distinctly lacking. But at least they could depend on the faithful Oxo cube (1945, page 18) to beef things up.

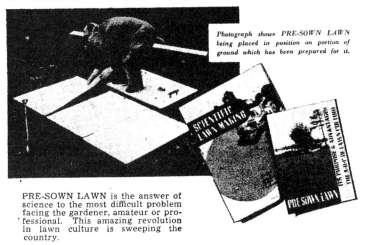

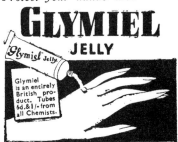